Cybertrips in Social Studies

Online Field Trips for All Ages

Scott Mandel

Tucson, Arizona

About Zephyr Press

Founded in 1979 in Tucson, Arizona, Zephyr Press continually strives to provide quality, innovative products for our customers, with the goal of improving learning opportunities for all children. With a focus on gifted education, multiple intelligences, and brain-compatible learning, Zephyr Press material is selected to help *all* children reach their highest potential.

Cybertrips in Social Studies
Online Field Trips for All Ages

Grades K–12

© 2002 by Scott Mandel
Printed in the United States of America

ISBN: 1-56976-145-0

Editing: Melanie Mallon
Design & Production: Dan Miedaner
Cover: Dan Miedaner
Illustrations: Stirling Crebbs

Published by:
Zephyr Press
P.O. Box 66006
Tucson, Arizona 85728-6006
800-232-2187
www.zephyrpress.com
www.i-home-school.com

All rights reserved. The purchase of this book entitles the individual teacher to reproduce some activity sheets for use in the classroom. The reproduction of any part for an entire school or school system or for commercial use is strictly prohibited. No form of this work may be reproduced, transmitted, or recorded without written permission from the publisher. Requests for such permissions should be addressed to Zephyr Press. The Internet is an open and rapidly changing system; websites may contain material inappropriate for children. Educational best practice indicates that an adult should preview all websites before sending students to visit them.

Library of Congress Cataloging-in-Publication Data

Mandel, Scott M.
    Cybertrips in social studies : online field trips for all ages / Scott M. Mandel.
        p. cm.
    Includes bibliographical references and index.
    ISBN 1-56976-145-0 (pbk.)
    1. Social sciences—Study and teaching—United States—Computer network resources. 2. School field trips—United States—Computer network resources. 3. Internet in education—United States. I. Title.

LB1584.7 .M36 2001
371.33'4678—dc21   2001024064

Dedication

This book is dedicated to my teenage children, Aliya and Asher, two of the most amazing people I have ever known. As an educator, they have been my personal inspiration and joy since they were born. My greatest pride has been watching them become excellent teachers on their own, as they have already started to share my joy of working with kids.

Contents

Acknowledgments vi

Introduction vii

Part One—Preparing for the Trip 1

   1. Taking an Online Field Trip 3
- The Importance of Experiential Education 5
- What Is a Virtual Field Trip? 6
- The Organization of This Book 8

   2. Integrating the Internet into the Classroom 11
- How to Use Virtual Field Trips in Your School Setting 12
- Scheduling the Field Trip 13
- Scheduling with Limited or No Internet Access 14

   3. How to Locate Material on the Internet 19
- Do Not Panic if the Site Is No Longer Working 21
- Search Engines and Directories 22
- General Education Websites 24
- Comprehensive Subject Matter Websites 25
- Guest Books 26

   4. Evaluation—How Do You Know It Was a Worthwhile Experience? 29
- What Is Evaluation? 30
- Matching the Evaluation to the Goals—The Core Component of Evaluation 32

   5. How to Set Up Your Virtual Field Trip 37
- Overview of a Virtual Field Trip 39
- Provide the Students with the URLs 42
- Bookmark the Sites 43
- Create an Original Web Page 43

Contents

Part Two—Taking the Virtual Field Trip   47

  6. Community Field Trips   49
- Ways to Adapt the Virtual Field Trips   50
- Virtual Field Trip 1: Families and Culture   52
- Virtual Field Trip 2: Jobs People Have   57
- Virtual Field Trip 3: Places People Live   62

  7. History Field Trips   67
- Ways to Adapt the Virtual Field Trips   68
- Virtual Field Trip 1: Your Individual State   70
- Virtual Field Trip 2: The Declaration of Independence   75
- Virtual Field Trip 3: The Civil War   80
- Virtual Field Trip 4: The Great Depression   86
- Virtual Field Trip 5: Ancient Greece   91
- Virtual Field Trip 6: The Crusades   96
- Virtual Field Trip 7: The French Revolution   101

  8. Humanities Field Trips   107
- Ways to Adapt the Virtual Field Trips   108
- Virtual Field Trip 1: Democracy   110
- Virtual Field Trip 2: The Homeless   115

Appendix   121

  A Quick Introduction to the Internet   122
- Servers   123
- Browsers   123
- Plug-ins   124
- URLs and Addresses   125
- Links and Bookmarks   128

  The Multiple Intelligences: An Overview   128
  Blank Template for Creating Your Own Field Trips   129

Bibliography   135

Index   136

Acknowledgments

Many people had a hand in creating this book, all of whom were indispensable to the process. First of all, I thank Jenny Flynn, who many months ago made a call saying that she enjoyed my website and wanted to know if I would be interested in writing a book for Zephyr. I also want to thank Melanie Mallon for her wonderful editing touch, which culminates in this work, and Dan Miedaner for his beautiful design and production work. Working with all of the people at Zephyr has been a wonderful experience.

I also thank a group of educator friends who read over my pages and shared their ideas, insights, and suggestions. In alphabetical order they include Melodie Bitter, Michael Fishler, Jennifer Jones-Heroux, and Robert Schuck. I want to especially thank Aaron Moretzsky, an assistant principal at my school, who used his long-time, well-appreciated English teacher skills in editing my pages. These people are some of the greatest educators of the Los Angeles Unified School District, and their help, support, and friendship is highly appreciated.

Finally, I want to thank the two million-plus users of my website, Teachers Helping Teachers, who have always inspired me to work towards the implementation of the Internet in all of today's classroom curricula.

—Scott Mandel

Introduction

The Internet may prove to be one of the saviors of today's educational system. It can supply an unimaginable amount of supplemental curricular material for even the poorest school. In just minutes it can provide a teacher with things for the students that used to take hours, days, or weeks to procure. The Internet can take the students on trips to anywhere on the face of this earth, under the seas, out in space, or back in time—and without having to pay for a bus. Most important, any teacher can take advantage of this amazing innovation, even if the school is not wired for the Internet.

> **The Internet can take the students on trips to anywhere on the face of this earth, under the seas, out in space, or back in time— and without having to pay for a bus.**

This is a book for teachers, by a teacher. My goal is to allow all teachers access to the wonders of the Internet, or as I call it, the ultimate teacher resource center. This book demonstrates how you can use the Internet to take students on curricular virtual field trips. Composed of two basic parts, the first half discusses the background of virtual field trips—what they are and why they are important. The chapters then take you through a step-by-step process for how to locate educational websites and how to integrate the material into your existing curriculum.

The second half of the book provides a dozen examples of actual virtual field trips that you can use as provided or adapt to the curriculum. The chapters cover every major aspect of the social studies and history curriculum from kindergarten through high school: the community, American history, world history, and the humanities. The topic areas of the individual trips come from the most traditional areas of the curriculum—those areas that standard courses will most likely cover (such as families and culture, the Declaration of Independence, and the French Revolution). Each field trip chapter includes suggestions and information on how to integrate the experience directly into the curriculum, how to adapt the material to suit each individual teacher, and, most important, how to change it in order to cover additional topic areas within the overall area of study.

Finally, the book contains an appendix, with background on how to use the Internet (for those teachers still uncomfortable with this technology), an overview of the multiple intelligences, and a blank field trip template you can photocopy and use to create your own field trips.

The ultimate goal of this book is to be as teacher-friendly and useful as possible, while at the same time to help integrate the power of this 21st-century educational innovation into every social studies and history classroom. Enjoy, and I'll see you online.

—Scott Mandel, Ph.D.

PART 1

Preparing for the Trip

- The Importance of Experiential Education
- What Is a Virtual Field Trip?
- The Organization of This Book

1
Taking an Online *Field Trip*

In This Chapter

- The Importance of Experiential Education (p. 5)
- What Is a Virtual Field Trip? (p. 6)
- The Organization of This Book (p. 8)

Search Engines   **Directories**   **Bookmarks**   **Internet**   **Cybertrips**   **Browsers**

Mr. Gonzalez's American history class was studying the Second World War. They had learned all about the important facts, major battles, catastrophic events of the Holocaust, and the various personalities and issues of the time. However, Mr. Gonzalez found that he could not get his students to understand or empathize with the culture of America during World War II. The students simply did not comprehend or relate to the concept of the war being the "last popular war," with the entire country mobilized and supportive of the war effort. Sure, he was able to teach about rationing, women in factories, sports stars enlisting, and the irrational fear and subsequent treatment of Japanese Americans. But his students simply did not get it. They could not relate to the way our society behaved during the early 40s.

To help his students better understand this period, Mr. Gonzalez decided to take them on a virtual field trip back to the America of the World War II era. He located a number of sites on the Internet that showed the students the culture of that time. He then drew a basic map of their community as it might have looked in 1943 (no highways, for example) and made hyperlinks for the students to follow as they "visited" various places on the map. Some of these stops on the virtual field trip included the following:

Dear Miss Breed—Letters from Camp
www.janm.org/breed/title.htm
This site is part of the Japanese-American National Museum and is filled with 250 letters that Japanese-American teenagers wrote from detention camps to a children's librarian in San Diego.

Propaganda Posters
www.openstore.com/posters
This site contains over two dozen propaganda posters that were popular during WWII, exemplifying the mood and ideals of American culture.

Radio Days: A Sound Bite History
www.old-time.com/sponsors/radiomemories//soundbytes.html
This site contains various selections from the most famous radio broadcasts of the era.

What Did You Do in the War, Grandma?
www.stg.brown.edu/projects/WWII_Women
This site contains interviews and stories of women and their roles in American society from factories to baseball.

Mr. Gonzalez's virtual field trip proved to be an overwhelming success. Throughout class discussions during the following month, the students continually referred to items and ideas culled from the experience. In addition, many of the students related that they had discussed life during this time with relatives who had lived through the war period. The students were able to ask questions, raise issues, and comprehend many of the aspects of American life at this time. Ultimately, the online trip to the America of World War II significantly raised the critical-thinking levels of the students.

The Importance of Experiential Education

From the earliest days of education, educators have maintained that students learn best when they experience the material, rather than learning it by rote memorization (Dewey 1959). This *experiential learning* can take place both within and outside the classroom. Field trips, organized educational experiences outside of the classroom, have been an important part of the curriculum ever since the days of the ancient Greek teachers Aristotle and Socrates (Krepel and Duvall 1981).

Field trips provide students with "the opportunity to go places where the materials of instruction may be observed and studied directly in their functional setting; for example, a trip to a factory, a city waterworks, a library, a museum, etc." (Krepel and Duvall 1981, 7).

Field trips, organized educational experiences outside of the classroom, have been an important part of the curriculum ever since the days of the ancient Greek teachers Aristotle and Socrates.

Field trips are not simply fun excursions outside the classroom setting. They have tremendous educational value. Recent studies show that field trips provide significant gains in students' cognitive and affective development. This is especially the case for urban, at-risk students (Rudman 1994).

Many schools today are discovering that securing approval for field trips is becoming increasingly difficult. This unfortunate situation can be directly attributed to two current trends in the contemporary educational environment:

- The current emphasis on standards. Field trips that do not *directly* address the curricular standards are disallowed.
- Reduced budgets that, in turn, reduce the number of field trips permitted.

A teacher can overcome the first of these problems, connection to the standards, through careful planning. As with all curricula, if a teacher can show that a field trip directly addresses the standards and directly affects student achievement, the activity can be justified and ultimately approved. The material in part 2 of this book centers on topics that are standard areas of all social studies curricula and would therefore meet this requirement.

> **A virtual field trip can take students anywhere in the world, to any time or place.**

The second of these problems, a lack of money, is not as simple to remedy. However, you can address this part of your students' experiential education through use of the Internet. How you, as an everyday classroom teacher, can easily integrate this new technology into the everyday classroom is the core emphasis of this book.

What Is a Virtual Field Trip?

Probably the greatest use of the Internet is as the ultimate teacher resource center. The teacher in the anecdote on page 4 incorporated this technology directly into his curriculum in order to take his students to a time and place that would have been impossible to visit. Through the use of modern technology, his students were able to see and hear things they could never have experienced with a textbook or normal supplementary materials. They were able to read and study primary source material that would have been impossible to use unless they visited a museum.

This new type of online curricular experience is called a *virtual field trip*. Similar in theory to an actual field trip, the experience takes the students outside the everyday classroom to experience primary source materials, and to use their senses to gain knowledge in a particular subject area. A virtual field trip can take students anywhere in the world, to any time or place. The trip can also take the students somewhere you would love to visit but cannot, due to time or money constraints.

Virtual field trips expand learning and understanding; they provide educational experiences that would have been unheard of ten years ago. In addition, they are relatively simple to construct and use. All one needs is an Internet connection.

Similar to traditional field trips, a successful and worthwhile virtual field trip has the following key elements:

- The field trip directly addresses the curricular goals of the teacher.
- The field trip involves access to visual representations of the curricular material, similar to having students look at material in a museum exhibit.
- The field trip provides a narrative at a level that each student can comprehend—similar to listening to a tour guide at a museum.

Before we go further, we should look at examples of previously constructed virtual field trips. (See below.) This will give you a feeling for the entire virtual field trip concept. Various educators and organizations created the following Internet sites as online experiences. Try a few of them to get an idea of what a virtual field trip encompasses. Simultaneously, consider how experiences such as these can enhance the classroom curriculum.

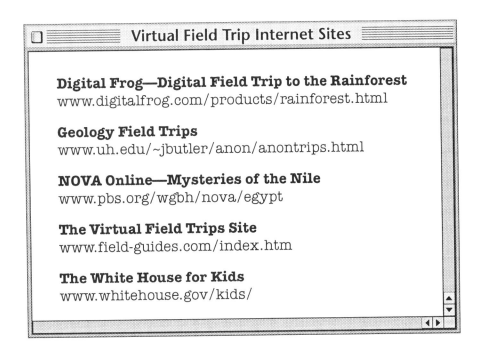

Virtual Field Trip Internet Sites

Digital Frog—Digital Field Trip to the Rainforest
www.digitalfrog.com/products/rainforest.html

Geology Field Trips
www.uh.edu/~jbutler/anon/anontrips.html

NOVA Online—Mysteries of the Nile
www.pbs.org/wgbh/nova/egypt

The Virtual Field Trips Site
www.field-guides.com/index.htm

The White House for Kids
www.whitehouse.gov/kids/

The Organization of This Book

Unfortunately, few virtual field trips are currently available, and most of those that are available revolve around the subject areas found within the sciences. For example, the Virtual Field Trips Site listed on page 7 currently includes about 15 field trips, and all of them are directly related to the science curriculum. The social studies and history teacher will find a minimal number of previously constructed field trip sites.

This book is designed to help you easily and quickly integrate a virtual field trip experience into your present curricula in two ways:

1. The virtual field trips are in standard content areas, so you can directly integrate them into the curriculum.

2. The field trips are adaptable to other topics. (For example, chapter 7 includes a field trip that explores ancient Greece, within the subject area of early world history. The introductory pages of that chapter list ways to adapt the field trip to a different culture within that era, such as Roman culture, including sites and search engines you can use to find more information.)

Following is an overview of the various topics and sections throughout the rest of this book.

Chapter 2: Integrating the Internet into the Classroom

discusses the various ways to integrate the Internet, and virtual field trips in particular, into your classroom, regardless of the physical layout of the room and school, including solutions to potential problems, such as scheduling the field trip and using outside resources. The material describes how you can incorporate virtual field trips into the curriculum whatever your school's online situation—whether it has a full computer lab, classroom computer pods, one classroom computer, or even situations in which your school has no Internet-compatible computers at all.

Chapter 3: How to Locate Material on the Internet

instructs you on how to locate various websites in order to adapt the virtual field trip to your particular curriculum, or how to update the trip if some of the published URLs no longer work or exist. The chapter concentrates on the steps to take in order to locate any online materials: how to use online tools such as search engines and directories, general education websites, comprehensive subject matter websites, and teacher guest books.

Chapter 4: Evaluation—How Do You Know It Was a Worthwhile Experience?

covers the entire concept of evaluation, both formal and informal. The chapter discusses the core components of evaluation, reviews how to match the evaluation to the goals, and provides suggestions for evaluating your own virtual field trip.

Chapter 5: How to Set Up Your Virtual Field Trip

explains the basic format of the virtual field trips in this book. The chapter also provides suggestions for the three basic ways you can present the online experiences to your students.

Chapter 6: Community Field Trips

includes field trips that concentrate on the various parts of the primary curriculum: family and culture, jobs people have, and the places people live.

Chapter 7: History Field Trips

focuses on the various areas of history found in the curriculum from elementary through high school. The overall subject areas in this section are state history, early American history (pre-1800), middle American history (1800–1900), modern American history (1900–present), early world history (B.C.E.), middle world history (0–1700 C.E.), and modern world history (1700–present).

Chapter 8: Humanities Field Trips

deals with the supplemental subject areas normally found in secondary education, including concept courses and social action.

Appendix:

Finally, the book concludes with an appendix that includes, for the inexperienced Internet user, a basic explanation of how the Internet works, introducing terminology that you will come across (such as servers, browsers, URLs, bookmarks, and links). The appendix also includes an overview of the multiple intelligences and blank forms you can reproduce and use to create your own virtual field trips.

For answers to these questions, read on in Chapter 2.

Integrating the Internet *into the Classroom*

In This Chapter

- How to Use Virtual Field Trips in Your School Setting (p. 12)
- Scheduling the Field Trip (p. 13)
- Scheduling with Limited or No Internet Access (p. 14)

Search Engines | **Directories** | **Bookmarks** | **Internet** | **Cybertrips** | **Browsers**

Mrs. Johnson's students explored the continent of Antarctica. They took a virtual field trip over the rugged mountains, studied the unique wildlife, and pretended to be geographers living on the barren land for three months.

Throughout the experience, the students learned about seasonal climate changes and what sections of the vast landmass were more hospitable than others. They studied the natural resources and the political problems resulting from various nations vying to take advantage of this huge mineral-rich continent. Upon completion of the virtual field trip, the students expressed how they thoroughly enjoyed the experience.

Mrs. Johnson works in a school where there is no Internet access at any computer, either in her room or in the computer lab.

How to Use Virtual Field Trips in Your School Setting

The definition of an educational utopia in the digital age is an Internet-connected computer at every student's desk across America, through which students can have direct online access at a moment's notice, any time, any day. Even one of these machines for every two to three students would be educational heaven. Unfortunately, to provide just one machine for every two to three students would cost $94 billion to purchase and set up equipment and another $27 billion annually to maintain (Dede 1997, 13). Obviously, this is not going to happen, especially in a society where educational spending is not a top priority.

How can we possibly hope to incorporate this technology into our classrooms if we have limited, or as in Mrs. Johnson's case above, no access to online educational resources? The answer lies in the various adaptations that you make to your computer situation. Regardless of your online status, you can still integrate the Internet into your curriculum, and students can still experience virtual field trips.

Internet access varies from school to school. However, unless you live in the digital utopia described above, your school most likely falls into one of the following four broad categories:

- A full computer lab with Internet access
- A classroom computer pod (3 to 5 computers) with Internet access
- One classroom computer with Internet access
- No Internet access at all

You can efficiently and successfully conduct virtual field trips in each of these digital situations. Obviously, field trips in some situations are easier to establish than in others. The next section reviews each of these potential school scenarios in the context of planning the virtual field trip and using outside resources to supplement classroom computer resources.

Scheduling the Field Trip

The baseline problem you will encounter, regardless of your computer setup, is time to finish the trip. Nothing is more frustrating for students engaged in a great online experience than to have to stop in the middle because they've run out of time.

Another problem, especially if you have a full computer lab, is having too much time for the particular trip. This situation causes classroom management difficulties when the students have completed the online experience and have significant lab time with nothing to do.

You may be tempted to schedule the trip as an assignment for students only after they have completed their class work, leaving it up to them how much time they have to take the trip. In this scenario, however, the slower students or those with academic problems will lose out on the educational opportunity, while the more academic-oriented students, or those who choose to rush through their work, receive extended on-line time.

Experience the Trip Yourself

The easiest way to avoid these problems is to experience each step of the trip personally. You can estimate how much time the average student will spend on the trip by knowing what curricular material the website includes and by knowing your students. Remember that the students' interest level is usually higher with online experiences than in the classroom. Consequently, round the time down to the lesser hour. It is always better to finish the trip a bit earlier than later.

> **A rule of thumb to employ is the more general the topic of a virtual field trip, the longer you can keep it on the computers because it remains relevant to the current curriculum.**

Be realistic about the amount of time available for the trip, the accessibility and speed of computers with Internet access, and the curricular goals you want to accomplish. You need to find a balance so the trip is both workable and successful for all of your students. A rule of thumb to employ is the more general the topic of a virtual field trip, the longer you can keep it on the computers because it remains relevant to the current curriculum.

Scheduling with Limited or No Internet Access

Virtual field trips conducted on classroom computer pods (three to five computers in the classroom) or on one classroom computer are definitely workable—if the students have sufficient time to conduct the trip. You will need to plan enough time for all students to experience the material. You can accomplish this in any or all of the following ways:

- Assign students specific times to work on the computers.
- Use an LCD projector for all or part of the trip.
- Use outside resources, such as students' personal computers or those in your community.

Assign Time Slots

To ensure that all students have equal access to the online experience, assign the students specific times to take the trip. Be aware that slower students who are scheduled to spend their work time on the virtual field trip may need additional time to complete their other class work. Basically, you need to find an acceptable and worthwhile compromise between the time required to experience the content of the virtual field trip and the realistic online access of your students.

Use an LCD Projector

Another alternative is to use a liquid crystal display (LCD) projector (or similar technology) with one classroom computer and take the students on a majority of the trip as a group. An LCD projector is similar to an overhead projector in that it projects the image from your computer screen onto a wall or area large enough for the entire class to view. The projector is actually smaller than a standard slide projector and hooks right into your computer.

> **Sample Schedule**
>
> If you have a classroom computer pod with five computers and a class of 32 students, you may make the following core decisions concerning the trip:
>
> - The online experience will take two hours to conduct thoroughly.
> - You can realistically expect a student to have thirty minutes of free work time a day.
>
> Taking these variables into account, you would need about six weeks for all of your students to conduct the trip successfully. This is not unreasonable for some of your larger units (such as the Civil War period). Obviously, for shorter trips, or for classes with fewer students, the time frame would be significantly shorter.

If you use an LCD projector to take the entire class on the trip at once, students can then do additional exploring on their own. This results in a situation similar to a real-life museum field trip, when a docent or teacher takes the class on a directed tour of the most important exhibits and then allows the students free time to explore the exhibits of most interest.

An LCD projector may have been beyond your school's means a couple of years ago, but the price has since dropped dramatically. Even if your school has only one or two projectors for the entire staff to share, you can plan in advance for its use, similar to scheduling time in a computer lab.

Use Outside Resources

As in the anecdote on page 12, your students can still experience a virtual field trip even if you have no Internet access at your school. Simply put, you need to be a little creative, along with developing a working knowledge of your community's online resources.

First of all, determine the number of students in your class who have Internet access at home. Assess this privately to limit social stigma between the "haves" and "have-nots." You can acquire this information quite easily by adding a question at the end of a test, such as "Do you have the Internet at home?"

Troubleshooting	
Potential Problem	**Solutions**
Not enough time for the trip	• Take the trip yourself and keep track of the time it takes. Use this as the basis for scheduling the field trip, with adjustments to allow for students' varying learning rates. • Be realistic: Consider students' online access and the time they have free. Adjust the scope of the field trip and the schedule accordingly. • Choose a broad curricular topic for the field trip so that it is relevant for a longer period of time, therefore giving students more time to take the trip. • Use an LCD projector to take all or part of the trip as a class. • Make the field trip voluntary.
Too much time for the trip	• Take the trip yourself and keep track of the time it takes. Use this as the basis for scheduling the field trip, with adjustments to allow for students' varying learning rates. Round the time down to the lesser hour. • Incorporate relevant learning activities to expand the trip.
Limited Internet access	• Assign specific time slots for each student to ensure all students have equal computer time. • Use an LCD projector to take all or part of the trip as a class. • Use outside resources: Privately determine students' home Internet access and then research free Internet access in your community (such as at a library or community center). • Make the trip voluntary.
No Internet access	• Use outside resources: Privately determine students' home Internet access and then research free Internet access in your community (such as at a library or community center). • Make the trip voluntary.

Next, locate community resources that provide free Internet access. For example, virtually every public library now provides this access. Many local religious institutions and recreation and youth centers are connected online and provide free access to those in the community.

When you finish accumulating information on student and community Internet access, you can determine how much material you must provide the students and how extensive the virtual field trip will be. (See chapter 5 for details on the process of creating this virtual field trip.) Obviously, the greater your students' access at home and at community locations, the more extensive the trip can be.

Problems with Using Outside Resources

Two potential problems automatically arise with using outside resources. The first is parental reluctance to allow the students to use the Internet by themselves at home or at an unsupervised community location. The second is the potential lack of access for some students to online resources—for example, issues related to the lack of transportation.

You can address parental concerns by asking the parents to conduct the virtual field trip with their child. This provides not only parental control, but also a wonderful family educational opportunity.

The second problem, access issues, is not as easy to address. If students have legitimate access problems, then you must ensure that the virtual experience is voluntary and a supplemental part of the curriculum. In other words, you must guarantee that you will not evaluate any aspect of the trip as part of the students' overall grade. (See chapter 4 for more information about evaluating virtual field trips.) To do otherwise would potentially penalize the students for their socio-economic status or for situations unrelated to their academic standing.

Chapter 2

You may not have the ideal Internet situation in your school, but as this chapter illustrates, you can take a virtual field trip regardless of your situation. You just need to adapt and make full use of the resources available in your school and community.

For answers to these questions, read on in Chapter 3.

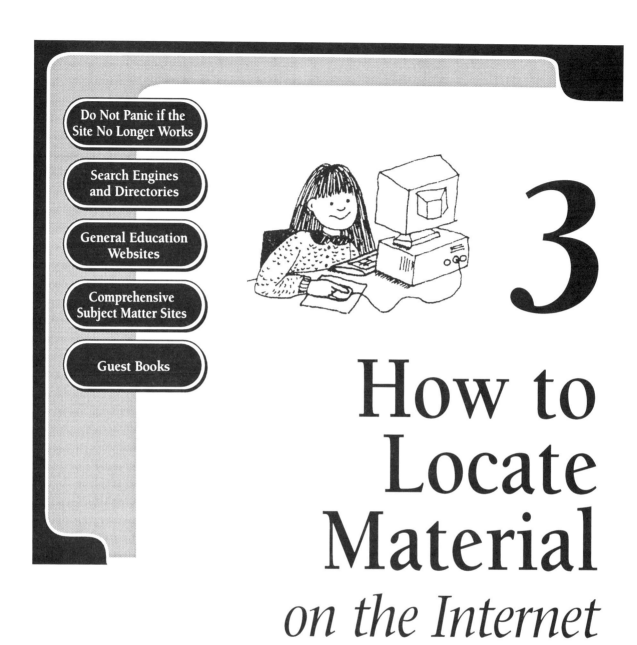

How to Locate Material *on the Internet*

- Do Not Panic if the Site No Longer Works
- Search Engines and Directories
- General Education Websites
- Comprehensive Subject Matter Sites
- Guest Books

In This Chapter

- Do Not Panic if the Site Is No Longer Working (p. 21)
- Search Engines and Directories (p. 22)
- General Education Websites (p. 24)
- Comprehensive Subject Matter Websites (p. 25)
- Guest Books (p. 26)

Search Engines   Directories   Bookmarks   Internet   Cybertrips   Browsers

Chapter 3

The yearly theme of Ms. Hughes's social studies curriculum was ancient civilizations. She was currently teaching about the Babylonian Empire and had reached the point where the class was discussing how standardized laws came into being during the reign of Hammurabi. During the course of the classroom discussion, Ms. Hughes pointed out how many of the laws that found their way into biblical-era texts actually had their origins in Hammurabi's Code of Laws. Unfortunately, the textbook only provided a couple of basic examples of this primary document, and the students were interested in knowing more.

Ms. Hughes went to the library resource center and unfortunately realized that no resources listed the Code of Hammurabi. Rather than spend hours searching for such a resource outside of the school, she decided to locate the material on the Internet.

She recalled an educational workshop she had recently attended that had provided a list of links to ancient civilization websites. Locating the handout in her files, she found a site that supposedly contained the Code of Hammurabi. She then went to a library computer and typed in the URL.

To her dismay, Ms. Hughes discovered that the Internet site no longer existed.

Refusing to panic or give up, Ms. Hughes went to a general education site. Once there, she scanned through the educational resources page until she came to the list of links for history and social studies. She soon found a link to The History/Social Studies Website for K–12 Teachers (www.execpc.com/~dboals/boals.html). Opening up the site, she quickly discovered a link to "non-Western history," which contained a link to a "Middle East" section, which in turn provided hundreds of sites related to the Middle East, past and present. Within minutes, Ms. Hughes located five different sites that contained material on Hammurabi's code. She selected the most comprehensive version, printed it, and brought it into her class for her students to study.

As teachers who regularly incorporate the Internet into their teaching will attest, the scenario above occurs quite often. The Internet is constantly changing and evolving. For this reason, published books and articles that list Internet sites, or handouts with lists of URLs, quickly become obsolete and useless. However, once you learn how to locate Internet resources quickly, you will be neither stymied nor frustrated as you search for good online educational materials.

Do Not Panic if the Site Is No Longer Working

As thorough as I try to be in this book you may experience two problems with the virtual field trips. These are the same problems that exist whenever you attempt to incorporate online material into your curriculum:

1. Some Internet sites will no longer work by the time the book or article is edited, published, purchased, and used.

2. You will need to adapt some experiences to better fit the particular subject matter of your classroom curricula.

Given this realistic assessment of current online educational opportunities, this chapter will teach you how to overcome both of these potential problems quickly and efficiently. Rather than discard one of the virtual field trips in this book because you require new websites, you can easily locate replacements or alternatives. In this fashion, the educational experiences in this book will remain relevant and operational for years. In other words, you will not be forced to recreate the wheel each time you use this material. Nor will you have to purchase new Internet books continually as sites become outdated, as is the case with many Internet resource collections.

People create thousands of Internet sites every day. A crucial fact to keep in mind is that hundreds of these sites have duplicate material. Remember, you need only one sample of material for the various sections of your virtual field trips. Here is an example of this concept: You need some information from an encyclopedia. Your school library has six different encyclopedias, and a couple of these have multiple editions (different publication dates). Do you look through each of them for the same data? Of course not. You select the one with which you feel most comfortable and which also provides the information that you require.

> **People create thousands of Internet sites every day. A crucial fact to keep in mind is that hundreds of these sites have duplicate material.**

The same concept applies when searching for Internet sites. For instance, if you are searching for a picture of the Roman forum for a virtual field trip to ancient Rome, you can easily locate dozens of pictures with a one-minute search. However, you need only one picture. The same is true of Internet sites. With this concept in mind, you'll find it's relatively fast and easy to locate additional Internet sites as replacements or as supplements to the Internet addresses listed in this book.

Your library resource center has various types of resources and materials—encyclopedias, books, and periodicals—specially designed to provide different types of information, each of which is more relevant to use at a particular time during research. For example, when investigating a topic, you may start with an overview from an encyclopedia, move on to an in-depth article in a periodical, and then go into greater depth with a book. Similarly, the Internet also has a number of tools that you can use in locating various types of online curricular materials. They are search engines and directories, general educational sites, comprehensive subject matter sites, and guest books. Following is a basic overview of the various types of mechanisms available for teachers to locate online curricular materials. For a more detailed discussion of these procedures, see *Social Studies in the Cyberage: Applications with Cooperative Learning* (Mandel 1999).

Search Engines and Directories

When looking for online information or materials, the first place to investigate is a search engine or directory. Directories categorize files by subject matter whereas a search engine sorts files by key terms. A search engine usually contains many more Internet sites than a directory does.

Dozens of search engines are currently available. Unfortunately, they all suffer from the same basic problem—when you ask for a search term, they give you everything they have. This can result in literally thousands of potential sites. Worse yet, the sites are not in any useable order other than the location and use of your search word within the site. Many of the sites may not even be relevant, if the keyword you used in your search has many different meanings and contexts.

> **Quality, not quantity, is the key when conducting an online search for curricular material.**

For example, you want to find a website with information about Zeus and the other Greek gods. Using the popular search engine Lycos (www.lycos.com), and the search term "Greece," you would receive over a million sites in your search. Obviously, this is a totally unmanageable number, considering that if you spent no more than two seconds scanning each description, it would still take you just under 30 days of reading,

24 hours a day, to go through all of them. Even if you limit the search term to "ancient Greece," the situation would not become more manageable. You would still have to wade through descriptions of more than 100,000 different sites.

A solution to this problem is to incorporate a search tool called a *meta-search engine,* such as Metacrawler (www.metacrawler.com). Other meta-search engines exist (such as www.dogpile.com) if you wish to experiment to find the right one for you and your students (or if, due to the ever-changing nature of the Internet, Metacrawler is unavailable by the time you read this book). A meta-search engine has no files of its own; rather, it searches all of the major search engines, and then it supplies you with a significantly smaller sampling of websites, usually 50 to 80. Using the term "ancient Greece" with Metacrawler, you would then receive fewer than 70 sites to scan through, a much more workable number. In fact, in this particular search, approximately one quarter of these sites has usable curricular material concerning the Greek gods.

Will you miss many potentially good sites using a meta-search engine rather than a traditional one? Of course. However, remember that you need only one site per topic. Quality, not quantity, is the key when conducting an online search for curricular material.

Directories, such as Yahoo! (www.yahoo.com), the most famous one, work in a similar fashion. This online tool, however, is extremely selective when listing and categorizing sites. Yahoo! is most appropriate to use when you require any sort of official site, such as a government site, or information about a well-known topic or person. For example, Yahoo! is ideal for students to research material on any modern countries or states. You would go to Yahoo!, select the "regional" category, then select either "country" or "U.S. states." Then all you would have to do is select the particular location you want, and subsequently, the subcategory (such as "history," "culture," "government," and so forth). Lists of relevant Internet locations on that particular subtopic are at your fingertips.

General Education Websites

All phone numbers are automatically listed with the telephone company's directory assistance service (unless the owner specifically requests an unlisted number). Unfortunately, the URLs of Internet sites are not automatically listed in all search engines and directories. The owners of a site must submit their URL to every search engine and directory to be listed at that particular location. Some of these search tools are quite strict in their criteria for inclusion; some list every URL that is submitted regardless of quality or subject matter. The end result is that other than those sites that are well known or connected to major corporations, few Internet sites are listed in each and every search engine and directory. In addition, many sponsors of educational sites—especially those created by teachers or students—do not submit to, and are subsequently not listed in, any of the search engines.

Therefore, the next place to turn to locate sites would be a general education website. A general education website contains lists of links to numerous other sites. It acts like an educational cybershopping mall. Consequently, instead of searching for various cyberlocations, you can go to one place and find virtually anything you need—your one stop for locating educational sites.

You should become familiar with two major general education websites:

> **Kathy Schrock's Guide for Educators**
> www.discoveryschool.com/schrockguide
>
> **Teachers Helping Teachers**
> www.pacificnet.net/~mandel

Both of these sites act in a similar fashion: They provide a number of links to the best educational sites on the Internet. Both sites also simplify your work by organizing the sites by subject matter. Kathy Schrock's Guide for Educators lists hundreds of educational sites. The educational resources page of Teachers Helping Teachers primarily lists educational Internet locations that cover large subject areas. The most important criterion for inclusion on this page is that each of the listings contains hundreds of additional links in that particular specialty area, thereby allowing you to locate your subject matter of interest on this resources page without having to wade through dozens of sites that may not interest you.

You should definitely bookmark (or add to your favorites list) both of these sites for continued use. Incorporating either one of these resources will lead to almost any educational link imaginable, which in turn will drastically limit search time on the Internet, because you can go directly to one of these two general educational websites and locate whatever you want.

Comprehensive Subject Matter Websites

Comprehensive subject matter websites operate in a similar fashion to general education websites. The difference is that they focus on one particular curricular area, be it social studies, language arts, math, science, or another area. As with the general education sites, these sites regularly include a multitude of educational listings with myriad subtopics. In addition, they list many sites, especially those created by students or teachers, that you won't find listed anywhere else on the Internet.

Without question, the most important comprehensive subject matter website in the area of social studies and history, and one every social studies and history teacher should bookmark, is the History/Social Studies Website for K–12 Teachers (www.execpc.com/~dboals/boals.html). This one location contains thousands of educational websites divided into more than two dozen easy-to-locate topics, including the following:

- American history
- European history
- Non-Western history
- Archaeology
- Geography and economics
- Religion, ethics, philosophy
- Research and critical thinking
- News and current events

In addition, all of these topics are divided further into easy-to-use subtopics. For example, the American history section includes the following subtopics:

- Colonial-Revolutionary
- Native Americans and the frontier West
- The Civil War
- Post–Civil War to 1900
- Migration and immigration sources
- Imperialism
- World War I
- The Depression
- World War II
- The Cold War and Korea
- Vietnam
- Recent
- Civil rights
- Ethnic, race, and gender issues

This one site will prove to be indispensable as you update or adapt the various virtual field trips in this book.

Guest Books

When you have seemingly exhausted your search possibilities, and you still are looking for a distinct type of site, turn to a teacher guest book. Guest books are different from bulletin boards—the most frequently used method of contacting other teachers online. Bulletin boards simply allow you to post questions and answers. Guest books, on the other hand, allow you to create a dialogue with other teachers by giving you a chance to respond personally through e-mail.

A frequently used teacher guest book can be found at the Teachers Helping Teachers site (www.pacificnet.net/~mandel). This particular teacher guest book is a vehicle for teachers to network all over the world. By simply clicking on the link labeled "add," you will view a simple form in which to type your name, city, e-mail address, and question. After clicking on the "submit" button, your question will be posted and teachers all over the world can answer you directly. Most submissions receive from three to 12 answers within 48 hours.

For example, in one of my searches for a particular type of website, I submitted the following question to the guest book:

> "I am searching for a website that gives me examples of Native American life in the Florida Everglades for a virtual field trip that I'm creating. Does anyone have any suggestions?"

Within 48 hours, I received seven responses. Five of the e-mails provided me with various URLs (two of which were completely new to me). One teacher gave me some new ideas for the virtual field trip, and one teacher offered to send me a unit she had created on the Native American tribes of Florida.

Using a teacher guest book is an easy way to network worldwide with fellow teachers, and to benefit from their expertise in creating or adapting your own virtual field trips.

The Internet is constantly evolving. Therefore any curriculum based on it—such as virtual field trips—must evolve as well. As you use the trips in this book, you may discover that some of the Internet sites no longer exist, and that some of the trips do not necessarily match your personal classroom curriculum. Again, do not panic. You can update or adapt any of the material in this book simply by using the preceding tools. With search engines and directories, general education websites, comprehensive subject matter websites, and guest books, you can quickly and effectively locate virtually any type of educational website you could possibly need. These easy-to-use Internet tools enable the virtual field trips in this book to be relevant, operational, and contemporary for years to come.

Chapter 3

For answers to these questions, read on in Chapter 4.

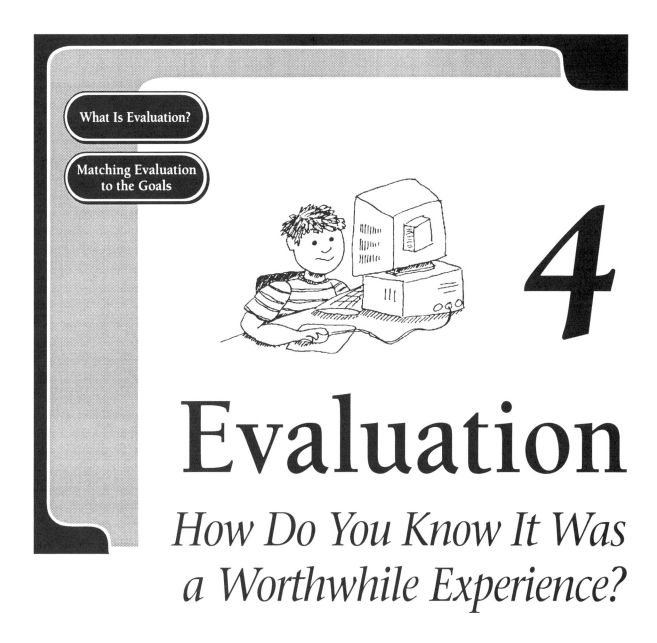

Evaluation
How Do You Know It Was a Worthwhile Experience?

In This Chapter

- What Is Evaluation? (p. 30)
- Matching the Evaluation to the Goals—
  The Core Component of Evaluation (p. 32)

Search Engines   Directories   Bookmarks   Internet   Cybertrips   Browsers

Chapter 4

Mrs. Ruela took her students on a virtual field trip to China as part of her seventh grade world history curriculum. After an opening online lesson during which the entire class visited certain key destinations of the field trip together, the students were left on their own to visit various areas of interest. Some of them spent time looking at the ancient sites. Some of the students investigated how the Chinese live and interact in different regions of the vast country. Still others looked at examples of Chinese culture.

Based on the fact that the students were both continuously on task and somewhat upset that they had to leave the computer lab, Mrs. Ruela thought that the virtual field trip was a worthwhile experience. It met her basic goal of providing the students with visual exposure to the various aspects of China.

Over the following two weeks, during classroom discussions on the China curriculum, Mrs. Ruela noticed that the students continually brought up examples of what they saw during their virtual field trip experience. Comments such as "On the computer trip, I saw . . ." or "We learned that on the Internet. It said . . ." became a recurring part of classroom discussions.

Even without a formal test or project, Mrs. Ruela ultimately arrived at the conclusion that not only were her students exposed to aspects of China they were currently studying, but they also had learned significantly—more than she expected—from the experience. As a result, she felt that the virtual field trip to China should become a permanent part of the China unit.

What Is Evaluation?

In today's test-score-and-standards-based educational atmosphere, evaluation has become an extremely important and controversial topic. Unfortunately, the word "evaluation" has become synonymous with "written test" or "graded project." In reality, as a teacher, you evaluate every day, usually without resorting to formal marks.

Educational evaluation is the way you determine how well something, such as an assignment, activity, approach, or behavior, has reached your goals. We have dozens upon dozens of goals in our classrooms. Some are written (such as state or district curricular goals), but most are not. All are aimed at creating a worthwhile, productive educational experience for your students, from the time that they enter until they leave the school.

There are basically two forms of evaluation:

- Formal evaluation
- Informal evaluation

Formal evaluation involves analysis of data leading to a mark, based on predetermined criteria. This can be a letter grade, a number grade on a rubric, or simple symbols such as a check mark, a happy face, or a pretty sticker.

Informal evaluation is based on the teacher's personal teaching repertoire. In other words, an informal evaluation comprises subjective decisions that are based on the teacher's professional experiences. These experiences then become a measuring stick to determine whether what you are evaluating (such as an approach or activity) has reached the established formal or informal goals. For example, if you showed a movie and class members visibly displayed their boredom throughout the experience, you may conclude that the movie was not suitable for your students and that you should not continue to incorporate it into your lesson plans. This conclusion is an informal evaluation based on observations of the students and knowledge of typical student behavior.

Both types of evaluation are critical to the successful operation of your classroom, and both are valid tools for measuring various aspects of your classroom curricula. In essence, teachers act as "educational connoisseurs," using their professional expertise to make value judgments about the worth of the learning experience (Eisner 1979).

> **All evaluation is simply a measure of particular goals. Whether your goals are formal, such as state or district curricular standards, or informal, such as wanting to expose your students to the material in a good video, you need to know what you want to accomplish and then evaluate whether you have accomplished it.**

Matching the Evaluation to the Goals—
The Core Component of Evaluation

> **The key to all evaluation is the opening definition:**
> Educational evaluation is the way you determine whether an activity has reached your goals.

The critical part of this definition is the last phrase—*your goals*. All evaluation is simply a measure of particular goals. Whether your goals are formal, such as state or district curricular standards, or informal, such as wanting to expose your students to the material in a good video, you need to know what you want to accomplish and then evaluate whether you have accomplished it. It really is that simple.

To relate this concept to your virtual field trip, you first need to determine its importance and position within the overall curriculum. There are a number of possible ways to view a trip:

- The virtual field trip provides core knowledge within the unit that every student must know.
- The virtual field trip provides material supplemental to the unit that will assist the students in their understanding of the overall principles.
- The virtual field trip provides an extracurricular activity for those students who want to explore and learn more, beyond what you present in class.

Each of these options leads to a different type of evaluation. The following section discusses each one of these possibilities as they pertain to your virtual field trips, and suggests the type of evaluation you need to meet the goals, including practicable general suggestions for each type of evaluation. (See also the chart on page 35 for a quick-reference guide to evaluating a virtual field trip.)

The Virtual Field Trip Provides Core Knowledge

If the goal of the virtual field trip is to provide important core knowledge for the unit, then you should formally assess the material to ascertain whether the students acquired the information. The important point to remember is that if all students must learn the material, then all students must have an equal opportunity to learn the material. This means that you must either present the material in a directed lesson as part of the field trip or require all students to visit a particular site and look at specified material. Under no circumstances should you make the material mandatory if students must take the virtual field trip outside the classroom or computer lab, or if every student does not have equal access to the classroom computers.

> **If all students must learn the material, then all students must have an equal opportunity to learn the material.**

General Suggestions for Evaluation

- Give a chapter or unit test that contains questions about the required material on the trip.
- Assign a project, graded by criteria on a rubric, requiring use of material from the trip.

The Virtual Field Trip Provides Supplemental Material

If the goal of the virtual field trip is to provide supplemental material to understand overall principles, then the evaluation should seek demonstration of the knowledge of the material. This implies that not everyone will use all or identical material on the field trip. You do not need to formally assess virtual field trips of this kind. If your goal is simply to supplement the curriculum, then you have to ascertain whether it has done its task, based on your personal goals and criteria for use.

General Suggestions for Evaluation

- Ask open-ended questions that determine whether the student learned material from the trip. For example, "Name at least one aspect of Greek daily life that you discovered while on the virtual field trip," or, "Name three things that a student of your age might have done in ancient Greece, based on your online experience." You can formally assess the answers to these questions if you do not insist that there is one "correct" answer, especially when the students may not have experienced the same material.

- Have students construct three-dimensional displays or a poster board incorporating material from the virtual field trip. Create a rubric to judge how well the students used the online materials.

- Observe the students and see how engaged they are while on the trip. Are they continuously on task? When it is over, do they want to spend additional time on the experience?

- Note how often the students introduce material from the virtual field trip into classroom discussions. Based on their use of this supplemental material, was it a worthwhile curricular activity?

- Interview a random sampling of students about the trip. Was it worthwhile? Did it keep their interest? Is it something they recommend for the following year?

The Virtual Field Trip Is an Extracurricular Activity

If your goal is for the virtual field trip to provide an extracurricular activity for those who want to learn more about the topic, then you need to provide opportunities for the students to demonstrate that the experience was worthwhile. This is the best type of virtual field trip goal if you have no Internet access at school and are leaving participation in the hands of the students and their families, outside of school time. However, under no circumstances should you hold all of the students accountable for *any* of the information from the trip, because not every student will have had equal access to the curricular material.

General Suggestions for Evaluation

- Have students construct three-dimensional displays or a poster board incorporating material found on the virtual field trip. Create a rubric judging how well the students used the online materials. Remember: You are assessing an extra credit project, not a mandatory project for all students.

- Note how often the students who took the virtual field trip introduce material from the trip into classroom discussions. Based on their use of this supplemental material, was it a worthwhile curricular activity?

- Interview a random sampling of students who experienced the trip: Was it worthwhile? Did it keep their interest? Is it something that they would recommend you use for your students the following year?

Matching Your Evaluation to Your Goals

Goal	Type of Evaluation	General Suggestions for Evaluation
The virtual field trip provides core knowledge.	Formal assessment to ascertain whether students acquired specific knowledge	• Give a chapter or unit test that contains questions about the required material on the trip. • Assign a project, graded by criteria on a rubric, requiring use of material from the trip.
The virtual field trip provides supplemental material.	Informal or formal assessment of whether students acquired knowledge of overall principles	• Ask open-ended questions that determine whether the student learned material from the trip. • Ask students to make three-dimensional displays or a poster board incorporating material from the virtual field trip, assessed by a rubric. • Observe the students and see how engaged they are while on the trip. • Note how often the students introduce material from the virtual field trip into classroom discussions. • Interview a random sampling of students about the trip.
The virtual field trip provides an extracurricular activity.	Informal assessment to determine whether the field trip was worthwhile for the students who participated	• Give an optional assignment: three-dimensional displays or a poster board incorporating material from the virtual field trip, assessed by a rubric. • Note how often the students who took the virtual field trip introduce material from the trip into classroom discussions. • Interview a random sampling of students who experienced the trip.

Chapter 4

Remember that evaluation doesn't have to be a formal test or lead to a mark. Virtual field trips are learning experiences for your students. As an educator, you need to incorporate what you know about teaching, learning, and your students to determine whether the virtual field trip was a worthwhile educational experience. The answer will ultimately depend on your curricular goals. Sometimes a formalized mark is appropriate. Sometimes all you need is a student to come up to you and say, "That was fun! Can we do another one?"

For answers to these questions, read on in Chapter 5.

- Overview of a Virtual Field Trip
- Provide the URLs
- Bookmark the Sites
- Create an Original Web Page

How to Set Up
Your Virtual Field Trip

In This Chapter

- Overview of a Virtual Field Trip (p. 39)
- Provide the Students with the URLs (p. 42)
- Bookmark the Sites (p. 43)
- Create an Original Web Page (p. 43)

Search Engines   Directories   Bookmarks   Internet   Cybertrips   Browsers

This chapter will help you decide the best way to approach a virtual field trip in your particular situation. The balance of this book (part 2) presents you with examples of virtual field trips in the most common topic areas of the social studies curricula, from kindergarten through high school. You may want to refer to part 2 as you read this chapter to help you decide the best approach for the field trips you plan to take with your students. The material in part 2 is divided by general subject matter, and the topics are mainstream—those that most teachers will cover within that curricular area. The field trip chapters break down as follows:

Chapter	Curricular Area	Virtual Field Trip Topic
6: Community (early primary grades)	Communities	Families and culture Jobs people have Places people live
7: History (late primary through secondary grades)	State history	Your state
	Early American history (pre-1800)	The Declaration of Independence
	Middle American history (1800–1900)	The Civil War
	Modern American history (1900–present)	The Great Depression
	Early world history (B.C.E.)	Ancient Greece
	Middle world history (0–1700 C.E.)	The Crusades
	Modern world history (1700–present)	The French Revolution
8: Humanities (secondary grades)	Concept courses	Democracy
	Concept courses	The homeless

Overview of a Virtual Field Trip

Each of the virtual field trips in this book has a set format that enables you to easily integrate the learning experience into the overall curricular unit. You can also incorporate this format as a guide if you create additional trips for your students throughout the year, or if you wish to adapt any of the current trips to your particular curricular situation. (See also pages 130–4 for reproducible blank forms you can fill in to create your own trip.) An abbreviated version of a field trip appears on pages 40–1 with descriptions of each of the field trip elements.

> **A more creative way to implement the experience is to put the sites into some form of package or structure, such as an itinerary for the trip.**

Unfortunately, you cannot simply plug this book into your classroom computer and experience the virtual field trips. The trips are complete and ready to use, but you need to put the material into a form that your students can use, and you may need to adapt the material to your classroom curricula. If after using some of these trips, you wish to create a virtual field trip from scratch, see *Virtual Field Trips in the Cyberage: A Content Mapping Approach* (Mandel 2000) or use the blank forms on pages 130–4.

You can prepare these field trips for your students in a number of ways, from the quick and simple to the more complex and time consuming:

- Provide the students with the URLs.
- Bookmark (or add to list of favorites) the sites on the computers.
- Create an original website.

All three possibilities will provide the students with a complete virtual field trip experience. Again, the primary difference is in the amount of time you wish to invest.

Overview of a Virtual Field Trip

- **Subject**—The broad curricular area explored on the field trip is identified here.
- **Topic**—The focus of the field trip is specified here.
- **Grade Range**—Adapt the material for your students within this range of grades.
- **Primary Objective**—Use or adapt this statement as your objective for the trip.
- **Subtopics**—Plan to visit these "stops" on the journey.

Subject: Early American History (pre-1800)

Topic: The Declaration of Independence

Grade Range: 5–11 (Adapt the material to the reading levels of your students.)

Primary Objective: As a result of this virtual field trip, the students will have a better understanding of how the events, personalities, and culture of the time period affected the writing and adoption of the Declaration of Independence.

Subtopics:
- Primary documents
- Important personalities connected to the signing of the document
- Historical Philadelphia

Integration into the Unit
This box suggests a focus for your learning activities before and after the trip, to help you make the most of the field trip within the unit.

Integration into the Unit

- Focus of learning activities before the trip: introduction to the Declaration of Independence; the Acts of Parliament concerning the American Colonies; the personalities most important to this event and era (such as Thomas Jefferson, Benjamin Franklin, John Adams, Abigail Adams, Betsy Ross, John Hancock, and King George III)
- Focus of learning activities after the trip: American and British responses to the Declaration; American symbols (such as the Liberty Bell, Statue of Liberty, and Uncle Sam); George Washington and the Revolutionary War

Time Frame for the Trip
The overall minimum and maximum hours for the successful completion of the experience

Time Frame for the Trip: 2–4 hours, depending on the age of the students and to what depth you want the class to investigate

Internet Sites
This chart lists all of the suggested sites for the trip, sorted by subtopic, including the title of the site, the URL (Internet address), and specific notes about the site. (Abbreviated version shown here.)

Internet Sites (Sorted by Subtopic)

Subtopic	Title of Site and URL	Notes about Site
Primary documents	**The American Colonist's Library** Personal.pitnet.net/primarysources	Look at the actual texts of all of the Acts of Parliament concerning the American colonies, especially the Tea, Sugar, Townshend, and Coercive Acts of 1774 (listed separately).
	Don Mabry's Historical Text Archive www.historicaltextarchive.com/links.php	Select "United States," then "Revolution," and open *Common Sense*, by Thomas Paine.
Personalities	**Lives, the Biography Resource** amillionlives.com	Look up biographies of Thomas Jefferson, Benjamin Franklin, Abigail Adams, John Adams, John Hancock, and King George III.

Graphic Organization of the Trip

Primary Documents
Text of Acts of Parliament
Drafts of the Declaration

Personalities
John Adams
Abigail Adams

THE DECLARATION OF INDEPENDENCE

Historic Philadelphia
Independence Hall
Landmarks and monuments

Modern Interpretations
Discussion of meaning of the Declaration
Broadway musical *1776*

Culture
Food
Songs and poetry

> **Graphic Organization of the Trip**
> Graphic representation of the relation of the subtopics and Internet sites (Abbreviated version shown here.)

Using the Multiple Intelligences

Intelligence	Activities
Verbal/Linguistic	• Read and discuss online material. • Write a story about one the founding fathers from the perspective of a family member, such as Thomas Jefferson's wife. • Create a dictionary that defines terms and slang of the period.
Visual/Spatial	• View images. • Draw a picture of an important event during the period. • Create a comic strip about one of the figures or events of the period.

> **Using the Multiple Intelligences**
> This table provides suggestions for addressing the eight multiple intelligences (see page 128) through the virtual field trip and in classroom activities resulting from the trip. (Abbreviated version shown here.)

Suggestions for Final Projects

- Role-play as delegates to the Second Continental Congress. Each student takes a different identity and researches his background and positions on various pertinent issues.
- View the movie musical *1776* and compare information in this historical movie with material on the virtual field trip.
- Report on colonial America. Suggested topics to cover: the history of the individual colonies, the British Parlimentary acts against the colonies, the colonists' responses, personalities of the period.
- Create a "*Time* magazine" of that period.

> **Suggestions for Final Projects**
> This is a short list of suggestions you can use to incorporate the material from the virtual field trip into a final project for the unit.

Provide the Students with the URLs

Providing the students with the URLs is the simplest way of presenting the virtual field trip to the students. At a minimum, all you need to do is furnish the students with the table printed in the Internet Sites chart (although you should check each site by taking the field trip yourself first). All of the URLs required for the trip are listed in their appropriate category. You can highlight any sites that are mandatory or recommended.

A more creative way to implement the experience is to put the sites into some form of package or structure, such as an itinerary for the trip. In this situation, you would create a narrative of some sort that guides the students through their experience.

For example, following is a narrative you could use with the Declaration of Independence trip (see page 75):

Itinerary

- The first thing to do on your trip is visit historic Philadelphia, where the Declaration of Independence was created, discussed, and approved. Take a tour of Independence Hall at **www.ushistory.org/tour/tour_indhall.htm**.

- When you are done, look at some of the other important buildings in Philadelphia at **www.nps.gov/inde/visit.html**.

- If you have some extra time, take a stroll through one of the beautiful old covered bridges at **william-king.www.drexel.edu/top/bridge/CB1.html**.

Creating an itinerary does not require much time, and it can help you direct the students to exactly where you want them to go, and focus in on exactly what you want them to see. You can also add questions or assignments along the way.

Remember also that even though this requires some time and planning on your part, whatever you create once can form the basis of future virtual field trips.

Bookmark the Sites

Bookmarking (or adding to your favorites list) the sites on the computers students will use is similar to providing the students with the URLs, except that you are providing them with the Internet sources directly on the computer. This requires a greater time commitment because you have to type each URL into the Internet browsers of either the individual computers or, if you are fortunate, a central server for a computer lab.

One way that you can expedite this process is to place all of the URLs that you plan to use into a file on a separate floppy disk. This way, you can simply cut and paste the URLs from the floppy onto the computer's Internet browser for bookmarking. If students use outside resources, you can provide each of them with a floppy disk that contains the URLs for them to cut and paste.

Rather than simply providing the students with the URLs for the virtual field trip, bookmarking them on the computer is an important task in two specific educational scenarios:

- The students are young (primary ages) and would have too much trouble typing in the URLs on their own. (Remember, in a URL, one tiny mistake means no connection.)

- You have limited time in a computer lab, so in order to provide your students with extra online opportunities, you bookmark the sites for them to use, thereby saving significant typing time.

After you bookmark the sites, you can create an itinerary for the students to use (see example on page 42).

Create an Original Web Page

This option takes the most work but is the most complete and fun way of experiencing the material. In this scenario, you create a graphic and place it online on either a school or personal web page. At specific points on the graphic, you create a hyperlink to the Internet sites that you are going to use. When the students click on a hyperlink, they go directly to the spot you want them to visit, as if they are actually taking a "trip" to different locations.

With today's technology, designing a virtual field trip web page is easy once you learn how. The technology coordinator at your school can recommend a web page design program and demonstrate how it works. (Adobe's web design programs are probably the easiest to operate—what you see on the screen is what you get on the designed page. The programs also come with excellent help files.) If you teach

> **The process of creating a virtual field trip web page and placing it online is actually quite simple. As an extra bonus, you can set up the page for parents to try during an open house.**

older students, many of them may already have web design expertise. All you have to do is provide them with the material and what you want to see on the page, and they can either assist you or design the page on their own as a classroom project.

Sample Web Page

Following is a partial description of how to build a web page for the Declaration of Independence trip (see example on page 45):

- Find a map of old Philadelphia, or draw a simple one containing all of the places to visit on the trip.

- Using the school scanner, scan the map as a gif file (a picture file that can be viewed on the Internet).

- Associate places on the map with locations on the virtual field trip: Independence Hall, a bulletin board or library for links to copies of the British Acts that led to the Declaration, a local house for the link to colonial food, a side picture of the Declaration for a link to modern interpretations. (Use your creativity to develop graphic representations of the sites.)

- Upload the completed page onto the school website. (The school technology coordinator usually does this.) If no school website exists, you can upload the page onto your personal website.

The process of creating a virtual field trip web page and placing it online is actually quite simple. It does take more time than providing a list of URLs or bookmarking them. However, as an extra bonus, you can set up the page for parents to try during an open house type of presentation.

This extended process is also a worthwhile investment when you consider that if you integrate the virtual field trip into your overall curriculum on a permanent basis, all of this work is finished for subsequent years. (You will need to verify that the hyperlinks still lead to active websites.)

Sample Web Page Map

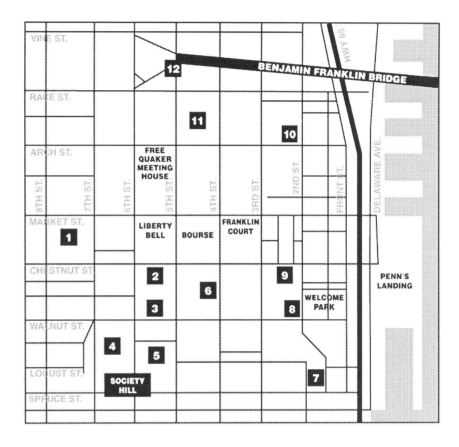

1 **Founding.com**
www.founding.com/gohome.htm
Start your trip at the **Graff house**, where Thomas Jefferson stayed while writing the Declaration of Independence. Select "The Declaration of Independence" for a discussion of the meaning of the document, including historical context, a glossary, a copy of Jefferson's rough draft, and more.

2 **Virtual Tour of Historic Philadelphia**
www.ushistory.org/tour/index.html
Take a virtual tour through historic Philadelphia, including **Independence Hall**.

3 **Don Mabry's Historical Text Archive**
historicaltextarchive.com/links.php
Take a breather in **Philosophical Hall** and learn more about the philosophy behind the Declaration. Select "United States," then "Revolution" and open *Common Sense*, by Thomas Paine.

4 **1776—The Musical**
www.geocities.com/Broadway/Wing/5800
Stroll through **Washington Square** for an outdoor musical performance: View pictures, download recordings, and read about the Broadway musical.

5 **The American Colonist's Library**
Personal.pitnet.net/primarysources
At the **Athenaeum**, a historic-site museum and library, take a moment to do some research. Use "find" to search the American Colonist's Library page for the British Acts of Parliament concerning the American colonies.

6 **Lives, the Biography Resource**
amillionlives.com
At **Carpenter's Hall**, where the First Continental Congress was held, sit a spell and learn about the various important figures of the era. Look up biographies of Thomas Jefferson, Benjamin Franklin, John Adams, Abigail Adams, John Hancock, and King George III.

7 **Loyalist, British Songs and Poetry of the American Revolution**
users.erols.com/candidus/music.htm
Time to take a break at the **Man Full of Trouble Tavern**, where you just might overhear some popular songs of the era.

8 **The Food Timeline**
www.gti.net/mocolib1/kid/food.html
Time for lunch! You have a reservation at the **City Tavern**, popular eatery among Jefferson, Washington, Franklin, Revere, and others. View recipes from the era, especially "dried apples from Paul Revere's kitchen" and "firecakes and pepper pot from Valley Forge."

9 **The National Park Service Independence National Historical Park**
www.nps.gov/inde/visit.html
Now that you've had a bite to eat, go to the **visitor center** and begin a virtual walking tour of Philadelphia's historic monuments.

10 **Betsy Ross Home Page**
www.ushistory.org/betsy/index.html
Betsy Ross has invited you to take a virtual tour of her **house**, read about her life, and learn about and view pictures of the flag.

11 **1777 Colonial Paper Money**
www.7cs.com/colonial/1777pa.htm
Visit the first **United States mint** and view pictures of colonial paper money.

12 **A Guide to Old Covered Bridges**
william-king.www.drexel.edu/top/bridge/CB1.html
On your way out of town, don't forget to enjoy the countryside, particularly Philly's **old covered bridges**.

Chapter 5

For answers to these questions, read on in Part 2.

PART 2

Taking
the Virtual Field Trip

6
Community
Field Trips

In This Chapter

- Ways to Adapt the Virtual Field Trips (p. 50)
- Virtual Field Trip 1: Families and Culture (p. 52)
- Virtual Field Trip 2: Jobs People Have (p. 57)
- Virtual Field Trip 3: Places People Live (p. 62)

Search Engines   Directories   Bookmarks   Internet   Cybertrips   Browsers

This chapter focuses on the curricula found in the early primary grades: kindergarten through third grade. (If you also cover local history, such as your city, refer to the material on the state history virtual field trip in chapter 7.)

The virtual field trips in this chapter are the following:

- Families and Culture
- Jobs People Have
- Places People Live

These three online experiences are general in nature, so you can easily adapt them to the individual curriculum of your classroom. (See Overview of a Virtual Field Trip, on pages 40–1, for details on the field trip format.) The most important step before taking your class on the field trip is to test the download time of the various sites on your school's server, so that you can avoid, or be prepared for, "dead time" as you direct the field trip experience for the entire class.

Ways to Adapt the Virtual Field Trips

You can substitute different subtopics and Internet sites to fit your students' background and your curricular goals:

- Choose to visit cultures and communities around the world that reflect your students' cultures (for example, a number of Korean students would lead you to include a virtual field trip to Korea).
- Choose different jobs and personalities as required by your specific district curricula or your curricular goals.

Finding Additional Information

The following website and search engines are good starting points for finding additional information on community topics and sites to include in your virtual field trip.

Community Topics and Sites

History/Social Studies Website for K–12 Teachers
www.execpc.com/~dboals/boals.html

- Select "American history," "European history," "general history," "non-Western history," or "diversity" to find information on communities and cultures during various time periods.
- Select "genealogy" for links to sites about families.
- Select "general history," then "people and the individual in history," for links to biographies and information on people in a variety of career fields.

Metacrawler
www.metacrawler.com

Type in a topic for the search. Select "phrase" for topics of two or more words.

Yahoo!
www.yahoo.com

Search using a keyword or follow the directory topics and subtopics:
- Locate material on famous individuals as representatives of different families or cultures.
- Look under "regional," then "countries," for links to sites about every country in the world. Each country has a subsection on the society and culture of that country.
- Look through the directory for Internet sites pertaining to the jobs you wish to explore. You might start with "business and economy," then select "jobs" to get a list of various fields (including a "cultures and groups" category). Look under "regional," then "countries," for non-American sources.

Chapter 6

Virtual Field Trip 1: Families and Culture

 **Subject** COMMUNITIES

 **Topic** *Families and Culture*

 **Grade Range** K–2

 **Primary Objective** As a result of this virtual field trip, the students will have a better understanding of what constitutes a family, and how the culture of the family affects their daily lives.

 **Subtopics**
- Different types of families around the world
- Different cultures expressed through art
- Different traditions in American society and around the world
- The immigrant experience

Integration into the Unit

- Focus of learning activities before the trip: definitions of family, culture, traditions, and immigration
- Focus of learning activities after the trip: the individual cultures of the students and their families; role of the individual within families

 **Time Frame for the Trip** 2–6 hours (teacher directed), depending on the depth of class investigation

Internet Sites

The chart on the following page groups the various "stops" on the virtual field trip by subtopic. As you plan for the virtual field trip, take the steps on page 54 to ensure a successful trip.

Internet Sites (Sorted by Subtopic)

Subtopic	Title of Site and URL	Notes about Site
Types of Families	The Amazing Picture Machine www.ncrtec.org/picture.htm	Search for "family," "mother," and "father" to get some pictures of people, animals, and plants. Review the pictures to select those most relevant to your class *before* taking the class on the field trip.
	Arctic Circle: Iñupiat of Arctic Alaska arcticcircle.uconn.edu/CulturalViability/Inupiat	View lots of pictures of and information about arctic Indians.
	The History Place—JFK Photo Library www.historyplace.com/kennedy/president.htm	Select from pictures of the president and his family. Click on pictures for larger image.
	Images of the American West www.treasurenet.com/images/americanwest/west007.shtml	Look through site for photographs of pioneer families. Click on pictures for full-screen images.
Culture in Art	African-American Art www.artsednet.getty.edu/ArtsEdNet/Resources/Maps/african.html	Examples of African-American culture through pieces of art. Site also includes discussion questions and activities for different grade levels.
	Art Touches the People in Our Lives www.artsednet.getty.edu/ArtsEdNet/Resources/Sampler/a.html	This site includes lessons incorporating art through which primary kids can learn how people have expressed their thoughts and feelings in art.
	Mexican American Murals—Making a Place in the World www.artsednet.getty.edu/ArtsEdNet/Resources/Murals/index.html	View examples of murals painted by Hispanic students and other artists in Los Angeles, expressing their culture and traditions.
	Navajo Art: A Way of Life www.artsednet.getty.edu/ArtsEdNet/Resources/Navajo/index.html	View examples of Native American culture through pieces of Diné (Navajo) art.
	Pacific Asian Art www.artsednet.getty.edu/ArtsEdNet/Resources/Maps/pacific.html	View examples of Pacific-Asian culture through pieces of art.
Traditions Around the World	Aka Kurdistan: A Place for Collective Memory and Cultural Exchange www.akakurdistan.com	View photographs of Kurds in native costume and read stories and information about Kurdish culture.
	Chinese New Year www.chcp.org/Vnewyear.html	View information about Chinese New Year traditions and links to pictures of New Year's celebrations.
	Christmas in Mexico www.mexconnect.com/mex_/feature/xmasindex.html	View pictures of various celebrations. Includes a number of stories.
The Immigrant Experience	New York, NY, Ellis Island—Immigration: 1900–20 cmp1.ucr.edu/exhibitions/immigration_id.html	View a collection of many pictures of the immigrant experience at Ellis Island.
	CET: Ancestors in the Americas www.cetel.org	View movie clips and pictures and explore the viewer's guide for information and discussion questions.

1. Take the trip first. Explore the various Internet sites yourself, before the students take the trip. This will give you a good idea of what material is covered, how appropriate it is for your students, and what learning adaptations you need to make, such as focusing on sites that suit your students' reading levels. You will also have the opportunity to time the trip and to check out physical aspects of the site, such as the need for plug-ins (see page 124) or extra time to download graphics.

2. Add, remove, or update sites. This is your opportunity to double-check that all of the sites are available. You may need to find alternatives. (See page 51 for information on finding alternative sites.) It is crucial for you to check the sites *before* your students begin the experience.

3. Study the chart organization. Note how the sites in the Internet Sites chart fit particular subtopics of the field trip. Adjust the subtopics and sites as necessary to suit your particular curriculum.

Graphic Organization of the Trip

The graphic organizer below demonstrates visually how the various subtopics and websites relate to the overall virtual field trip. You may want to recreate or photocopy this chart for your students before they take the trip. (A blank form is provided on page 132.)

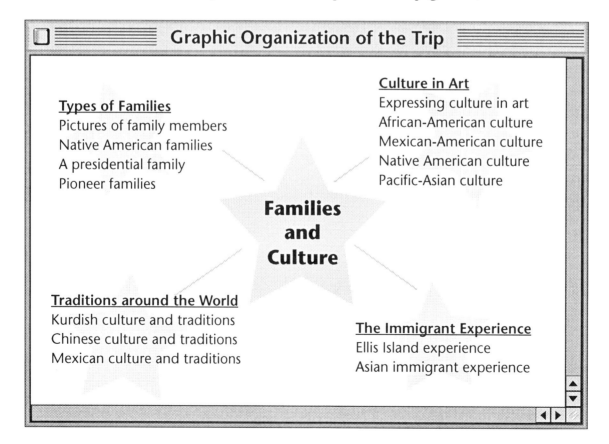

The Multiple Intelligences

The chart on page 56 is a tool to help you integrate the multiple intelligences into your curricular unit. The chart provides you with a list of specific ways to use the multiple intelligences before, during, and after the virtual field trip. (See page 128 for a description of the multiple intelligences.) Please note these are teaching suggestions, not mandates. You should choose what you have time for and what is appropriate for your class. You can also use these suggestions as a springboard for additional ideas.

Suggestions for Final Projects

- Have grandparents or other family members of the students come into the classroom and share aspects of their culture. Use the information to create personalized family scrapbooks.

- Have an international day, week, or month during which the students present and learn about other cultures and experience various cultural music, food, dance, and so forth.

Using the Multiple Intelligences	
Intelligence	Activities
Verbal/ Linguistic	• Read and discuss online material. • Share thoughts about and interpretations of art. • Read aloud letters from immigrants. • Read aloud stories about Christmas in Mexico or other holidays in different cultures.
Logical/ Mathematical	• Explore various items and information from the trip, discussing how immigrant families experience cultural change after settling in America. • Look for patterns in the various art examples. • Collect and play board games from around the world. • Look for geometric shapes in quilts, kenta cloths, tartans, and other cloth patterns from around the world.
Visual/ Spatial	• Use the same cloth patterns to look for common and individual visual themes. • Create your own "quilts" on paper. • Look at examples of visual written languages, such as Chinese, and practice creating ideographs. • View images on the trip. • Visualize what it would be like to grow up in a different culture or time period. • Create a montage of images from a particular culture. • Bring in and share family photographs.
Bodily/ Kinesthetic	• Learn a dance from one of the cultures studied. • Pretend to be one of the people encountered on the trip, such as an immigrant or someone from a different culture. • Play a physical game from one of the cultures. • Act out the scenes depicted in various pieces of art.
Musical/ Rhythmic	• Learn a song from one of the cultures. • Create a song about one of the cultures or people students encounter on the trip. • Learn about the musical instruments of different cultures. • Listen to music from different cultures.
Interpersonal	• Work as a group within the unit. • Divide into small groups, each representing one of the cultures, and take turns presenting information about each culture. • Conduct interviews in pairs, with one student as a member of a culture (or a specific person encountered on the trip) and the other student as the interviewer. • In small groups, make up the stories behind the different pieces of art.
Intrapersonal	• Discuss individual, personal aspects of culture. (Students can think about this issue and bring items that represent their cultures to class.) • Keep a journal of feelings and impressions about the field trip, using words or images. • Write or use pictures to create an "autobiography" from the perspective of an immigrant or member of another culture. ("If I were Kurdish, this is what my life might be like.") • Compare traditions of other cultures to students' own family traditions.
Naturalist	• Make a timeline of when the students' families came to America. • Create personal family trees. • Discuss the natural setting (geography, climate, and so forth) of various cultures and how it influences their traditions and identities. • Discuss the role of nature in various pieces of art and in different cultures. • Use natural art materials (plant dyes, stones, quills, and so forth) from different cultures to create art and compare with the original art of the culture.

Virtual Field Trip 2: Jobs People Have

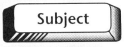 **Subject** — **COMMUNITIES**

 **Topic** — *Jobs People Have*

 **Grade Range** — 1–3

 **Primary Objective** — As a result of this virtual field trip, the students will have a better understanding of different types of jobs that people have in American society.

 **Subtopics**
- Public service providers
- American officials
- Professional specialties
- Famous personalities

Integration into the Unit

- Focus of learning activities before the trip: how communities operate and the types of jobs people have

- Focus of learning activities after the trip: more in-depth investigation into the various jobs on the trip and perhaps a look at a number of jobs not covered by the trip; follow through with e-mail to the public service providers

 **Time Frame for the Trip** — 2–6 hours (teacher directed), depending on the depth of class investigation

Internet Sites

The chart on the next page groups the various "stops" on the virtual field trip by subtopic. As you plan for the virtual field trip, take the steps on page 59 to ensure a successful trip.

Internet Sites (Sorted by Subtopic)

Subtopic	Title of Site and URL	Notes about Site
Public Service Providers	Web66: International School Website Registry web66.coled.umn.edu/schools.html	Find links to school websites all over the world. Select some and look at pictures of teachers and other school personnel. You can e-mail staff members with questions about the jobs they do.
	Yahoo!—Fire Departments dir.yahoo.com/Health/Public_Health_and_Safety/Fire_Protection/Fire_Departments/By_Region/U_S__States/	Select various states for lists of fire-department home pages around the country. You can e-mail sites with questions about the jobs people there do.
	Yahoo!—Police Departments http://dir.yahoo.com/Society_and_Culture/Crime/Law_Enforcement/Law_Enforcement_Departments/Local_Departments/Police	Select from home pages of hundreds of police departments around the country. You can e-mail sites with questions about the jobs people there do.
American Officials	American Presidents: Life Portraits www.americanpresidents.org/gallery	Click on a presidential portrait to see a larger image. Select a president from the "Pick a President" bar at the top of the page to see more information about each president.
Professional Specialties	Doctors of the World www.doctorsoftheworld.org	Select pictures of doctors helping people all over the world.
	Jelly Belly Factory Tour www.jellybelly.com/newhome/virtual_tour.html	Take a tour of the Jelly Belly factory.
	The News: The Process behind the Presentation library.thinkquest.org/18764/	Click on "broadcast journalism" for a behind-the-scenes tour of a real news studio (with short descriptions of who works there and what they do) or choose "printed news" and take a tour of a real newsroom. (Note: As a student-created site, it may not exist by the time you read this book. Search Yahoo! categories—www.yahoo.com—or use Metacrawler to find a replacement.)
Famous Personalities	Major League Baseball.Com www.majorleaguebaseball.com	Select from various pictures of major league baseball players.
	Lives, the Biography Resource amillionlives.com	Read biographies of people who have made a difference. Pick those that suit your curriculum. The site includes biographies and links grouped by profession.

1. Take the trip first. Explore the various Internet sites yourself, before the students take the trip. This will give you a good idea of what material is covered, how appropriate it is for your students, and what learning adaptations you need to make, such as focusing on sites that suit your students' reading levels. You will also have the opportunity to time the trip and to check out physical aspects of the site, such as the need for plug-ins (see page 124) or extra time to download graphics.

2. Add, remove, or update sites. This is your opportunity to double-check that all of the sites are available. You may need to find alternatives. (See page 51 for information on finding alternative sites.) It is crucial for you to check the sites *before* your students begin the experience.

3. Study the chart organization. Note how the sites in the Internet Sites chart fit particular subtopics of the field trip. Adjust the subtopics and sites as necessary to suit your particular curriculum.

Graphic Organization of the Trip

The graphic organizer below demonstrates visually how the various subtopics and websites relate to the overall virtual field trip. You may want to recreate or photocopy this chart for your students before they take the trip.

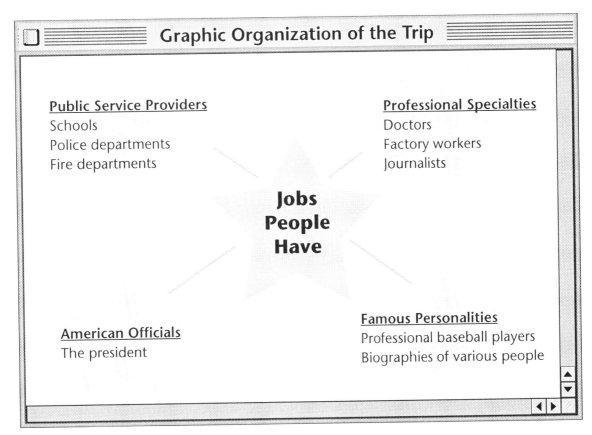

Chapter 6

The Multiple Intelligences

The chart on page 61 is a tool to help you integrate the multiple intelligences into your curricular unit. The chart provides you with a list of specific ways to use the multiple intelligences before, during, and after the virtual field trip. (See page 128 for a description of the multiple intelligences.) Please note these are teaching suggestions, not mandates. You should choose what you have time for and what is appropriate for your class. You can also use these suggestions as a springboard for additional ideas.

Suggestions for Final Projects

- Create a model of a community, based on the types of jobs that the students feel are important in a community.
- Create classroom jobs based on the requirements that the students feel are important for the smooth operation of the classroom.
- Have parents speak to the class about their jobs. Ask students to respond with essays or artwork that describe the job most interesting to them.
- Arrange for each student to talk to someone—in person or via e-mail—who has the type of job that the student would like to pursue one day and have him or her write a report on that job.

Using the Multiple Intelligences

Intelligence	Activities
Verbal/ Linguistic	• Read and discuss online material. • Create riddles and trivia questions about the jobs being investigated. • Discuss letters or important speeches of presidents.
Logical/ Mathematical	• Explore various items and information from the trip, discussing the connection between the jobs people have and the needs of the community. • Create a want ad for a particular job (without naming the job itself) and see if other students can guess what the job is. • Talk about how to pursue a dream job: What kind of education would you need? What are the best extracurricular activities to pursue?
Visual/ Spatial	• View images on the trip. • Visualize what the world would be like if one of the jobs (such as firefighter) did not exist. • Draw a picture of someone working in a specific field. • Locate on a map the schools, police departments, and fire departments from the field trip.
Bodily/ Kinesthetic	• Act out aspects of some of the jobs. • Play a game of charades using names of jobs. • Learn a skill (such as taking someone's pulse) that relates to a job. • Discuss jobs that require a great deal of physical skill (such as dance, sports, construction work).
Musical/ Rhythmic	• Explore music-related jobs in the community. • Make up a song about a job. • Discuss or write about the lives of famous musicians. • Listen to theme songs from TV shows about jobs and discuss how the songs make the students feel about the job, and whether the job has characteristics found in the music.
Interpersonal	• Work as a group within the unit. • Pick a job from the field trip and, in groups, take turns interviewing each other about these jobs. • Create a human assembly line to accomplish a specific task.
Intrapersonal	• Reflect on types of jobs each student may want to pursue one day. • List all the features of a dream job (such as ideal hours, location, daily tasks). • Write an "If I were a . . ." essay about one of the jobs on the trip or draw a picture of yourself doing a job. • Discuss or write about personal likes and dislikes in relation to one or more jobs on the trip.
Naturalist	• Create an idea web or Mind Map of the types of jobs that are needed in a community. • Discuss jobs that involve the natural world, such as park ranger, geologist, ecologist, or zoo caretaker. • Write about a famous person who works in nature.

Chapter 6

Virtual Field Trip 3: Places People Live

 **COMMUNITIES**

 *Places People Live*

 1–3

 As a result of this virtual field trip, the students will have a better understanding of the various types of communities and cultures that exist in the United States and the world, including those where the students' families originated.

- Your local community
- Nontraditional U.S. communities
- Latin American communities
- Communities around the world

Integration into the Unit

- Focus of learning activities before the trip: what constitutes a community; the community students live in; types of communities their families came from
- Focus of learning activities after the trip: actual field trips or more in-depth discussion of their own community; cultural aspects of various communities; communities not covered during the trip

 2–6 hours (teacher directed), depending on the depth of class investigation

Internet Sites

The chart on the following page groups the various "stops" on the virtual field trip by subtopic. As you plan for the virtual field trip, take the steps on page 64 to ensure a successful trip.

Internet Sites (Sorted by Subtopic)

Subtopic	Title of Site and URL	Notes about Site
Your Local Community	Yahoo! local.yahoo.com	Select your state, then your city. Browse until you locate some pictures of the community that you want to share with your students. The "community and culture" and "recreation and sports" links are good starting points.
Non-traditional U.S. Communities	Desert USA www.desertusa.com/life.html 360° Alaska in Panorama www.360alaska.com Virtually Hawaii hawaii.ivv.nasa.gov/space/hawaii/virtual.field.trips.html	Select from links to "people and cultures," "animals and wildlife," and "plants/wildflowers." View 360-degree panoramas of the entire state of Alaska, divided by region. Take a virtual field trip throughout the Hawaiian islands.
Latin American Communities	Amazon Interactive www.eduweb.com/rainforest/mestizo.html National Geographic: Discovering Mexico www.nationalgeographic.com/features/96/mexico	This comprehensive site tells about the various groups who live or have lived in the Amazon rainforest. Take pictorial tours all over Mexico.
Communities around the World	Kibbutz Ketura textstore.co.il/ketura Republic of Ghana—Scenes from Ghana www.ghana.com/republic/scenes/index.html	View pictures and information; and take a virtual bus tour of an Israeli kibbutz. View pictures and information on culture in West Africa.

1. Take the trip first. Explore the various Internet sites yourself, before the students take the trip. This will give you a good idea of what material is covered, how appropriate it is for your students, and what learning adaptations you need to make, such as focusing on sites that suit your students' reading levels. You will also have the opportunity to time the trip and to check out physical aspects of the site, such as the need for plug-ins (see page 124) or extra time to download graphics.

2. Add, remove, or update sites. This is your opportunity to double-check that all of the sites are available. You may need to find alternatives. (See page 51 for information on finding alternative sites.) It is crucial for you to check the sites *before* your students begin the experience.

3. Study the chart organization. Note how the sites in the Internet Sites chart fit particular subtopics of the field trip. Adjust the subtopics and sites as necessary to suit your particular curriculum.

Graphic Organization of the Trip

The graphic organizer below demonstrates visually how the various subtopics and websites relate to the overall virtual field trip. You may want to recreate or photocopy this chart for your students before they take the trip.

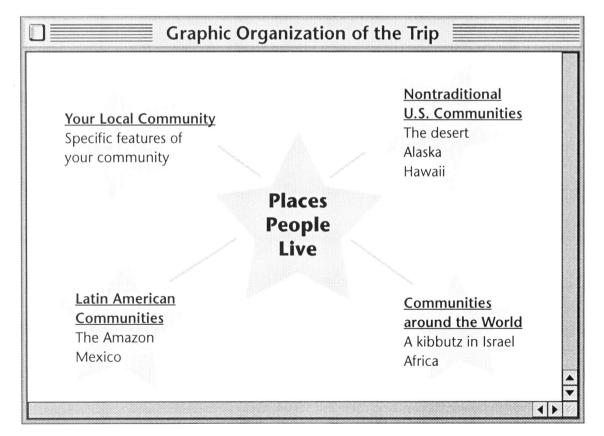

The Multiple Intelligences

The chart on the following page is a tool to help you integrate the multiple intelligences into your curricular unit. The chart provides you with a list of specific ways to use the multiple intelligences before, during, and after the virtual field trip. (See page 128 for a description of the multiple intelligences.) Please note these are teaching suggestions, not mandates. You should choose what you have time for and what is appropriate for your class. You can also use these suggestions as a springboard for additional ideas.

Suggestions for Final Projects

- Create a model of a community either on an individual level, in a small group, or as an entire class project.

- Write or give an oral report on your place in the community or where you would like to live.

- Come up with questions as a class and interview parents or grandparents about what it was like living in their community while they were growing up.

Chapter 6

\multicolumn{2}{c}{**Using the Multiple Intelligences**}	
Intelligence	Activities
Verbal/ Linguistic	• Read and discuss online material. • Take turns reading aloud the text that accompanies pictorial tours. • Make up a story about traveling to one of the places on the field trip. • Write or e-mail penpals in one of the places studied. (See the Teachers Helping Teachers guest book at www.pacificnet.net/~mandel for help finding penpals.) • Learn a word or phrase from the languages spoken in the Amazon, Ghana, Mexico, and Israel.
Logical/ Mathematical	• Explore various items and information from the trip, possibly manipulating data and materials in a final project or discussion. • Compare and contrast different communities on the trip. • Create a game with clues that describe a particular community or culture. • Compare and contrast the past and present details of a community or culture.
Visual/ Spatial	• View images, looking at examples of culture through art. • Create a travel brochure for one of the places on the trip. • Find each of the communities on a map. • Create a local community montage.
Bodily/ Kinesthetic	• Learn a traditional dance of one of the cultures. • Demonstrate a custom of one of the cultures on the trip. • Act as a tour guide of the local community. • Pretend to be from another culture while other students guess which one.
Musical/ Rhythmic	• Listen to traditional music of one of the cultures. • Learn a song from another culture. • Create a song about a culture or community. • Discuss the importance and flavor of music in the local community.
Interpersonal	• Work as a group within the unit. • In small groups, create trivia games about places on the trip for other groups to play. • Discuss how one culture might approach a problem in the local community. • In small groups, discuss places students have lived or visited.
Intrapersonal	• Write about or discuss personal feelings about the local community. • Write about or discuss personal answers to the question, "If you could live anywhere in the world, where would you live?" • Make individual choices during personal exploration time on the trip, or through opportunities provided by the teacher for personal choice or sharing of one's family culture.
Naturalist	• Make a chart of the various aspects and components of a community. • Discuss the plant and animal life of the regions on the field trip. • Write about or draw a made-up animal that might live in one of the regions on the trip. • Discuss the influence of climate and geography on various cultures.

7 History Field Trips

In This Chapter

- Ways to Adapt the Virtual Field Trips (p. 68)
- Virtual Field Trip 1: Your Individual State (p. 70)
- Virtual Field Trip 2: The Declaration of Independence (p. 75)
- Virtual Field Trip 3: The Civil War (p. 80)
- Virtual Field Trip 4: The Great Depression (p. 86)
- Virtual Field Trip 5: Ancient Greece (p. 91)
- Virtual Field Trip 6: The Crusades (p. 96)
- Virtual Field Trip 7: The French Revolution (p. 101)

Search Engines   Directories   Bookmarks   Internet   Cybertrips   Browsers

This chapter focuses on the curricula generally taught in the upper elementary and secondary grades. The virtual field trips in this chapter include the following topics:

- State History (your individual state)
- The Declaration of Independence (early American history, pre-1800)
- The Civil War (middle American history, 1800–1900)
- The Great Depression (modern American history, 1900–present)
- Ancient Greece (early world history, B.C.E.)
- The Crusades (middle world history, 0–1700 C.E.)
- The French Revolution (modern world history, 1700–present)

The most important point of concern is the academic level of your students. For example, American history is traditionally taught in some form in fifth, eighth, and eleventh grades. Although the Internet sites included on the virtual field trip are general in nature, you may need to adapt the material to the reading level and sophistication of your students. Take care not to use Internet sites that are either too difficult or too easy. (See Overview of a Virtual Field Trip, on page 39, for details on the field trip format.)

Ways to Adapt the Virtual Field Trips

You can substitute different subtopics in any of the field trips to match other goals in your curriculum:

- Focus on a different period in history, concentrating on historic documents, history of that time, personalities, and culture.
- Focus on different cultures within the same period of history, such as Roman or Babylonian cultures in early world history. Be aware that the available online material grows or shrinks depending on how old or well known the culture is. Use the given subtopics to guide your search for websites.

Finding Additional Information

The following websites and search engines are good starting points for finding additional information on history topics and sites to include in your virtual field trip.

History Topics and Sites

History/Social Studies Website for K–12 Teachers
www.execpc.com/~dboals/boals.html
- American history field trips: Select "American history" and then the time period in which you are interested.
- World history field trips: Select "European history" or "non-Western history," then a subcategory, such as "ancient and classical" in the former or "Middle East" in the latter.

Don Mabry's Historical Text Archive
www.historicaltextarchive.com/links.php
- American history field trips: Select "United States" then the appropriate area, such as "Colonial," "Revolution," or "Wars."
- World history field trips: Select "Europe" or "Asia," then a subcategory.

The American Civil War Homepage
sunsite.utk.edu/civil-war/warweb.html
Select areas of interest.

New Deal Network: A Guide to the Great Depression of the 1930s
newdeal.feri.org
Select areas of interest.

Metacrawler
www.metacrawler.com
Type in a topic for the search. Select "phrase" for topics of two or more words.

Yahoo!
www.yahoo.com
- State history field trip: Select "regional," then "U.S. states."
- American history field trips: Select "regional," then "U.S. states" for events in specific areas.
- World history field trips: Select "regional," then "regions," then the region of choice. Scroll down and select "social science," then "history."

Virtual Field Trip 1: Your Individual State

STATE HISTORY

Your Individual State

3–5

As a result of this virtual field trip, the students will have a better understanding of the many facets of the state in which they live.

Please note: Compared to the other virtual field trips in this book, this particular experience is rather incomplete. Unlike the other curricular topics that vary minimally from school district to school district, this virtual field trip has potentially fifty different representations (or more, if you adapt this trip to a province or other government unit). Therefore, the outline of the trip is in place for you to complete, based on the individual curricular goals of your school district. The URLs in the Internet Sites chart are general URLs that include multiple links to Internet sites for each state, thereby allowing you to choose relevant material for your unique virtual field trip.

Adapt these topics as necessary to fit your particular state and the goals of your curriculum.

- The geography of your state
- Cities in your state
- The history of your state
- Cultural aspects of your state
- Famous personalities who either grew up or worked in your state
- Important documents in your state history

> **Integration into the Unit**
>
> - Focus of learning activities before the trip: To be determined based on the goals of your curriculum, and the Internet sites you choose to visit. You might send away for materials about your state and learn about the subtopics to some degree before the trip.
>
> - Focus of learning activities after the trip: To be determined based on the goals of your curriculum, and the Internet sites you choose to visit. You might focus on particular cities in your state or learn about another state.

2–4 hours, depending on the age of the students and the depth of class investigation

Internet Sites

The chart on the following page groups the various "stops" on the virtual field trip by subtopic. As you plan for the virtual field trip, take the following steps to ensure a successful trip.

1. Take the trip first. Explore the various Internet sites yourself, before the students take the trip. This will give you a good idea of what material is covered, how appropriate it is for your students, and what learning adaptations you need to make, such as focusing on sites that suit your students' reading levels. You will also have the opportunity to time the trip and to check out physical aspects of the site, such as the need for plug-ins (see page 124) or extra time to download graphics.

2. Add, remove, or update sites. This is your opportunity to double-check that all of the sites are available. You may need to find alternatives. (See page 69 for information on finding alternative sites.) It is crucial for you to check the sites *before* your students begin the experience.

3. Study the chart organization. Note how the sites in the Internet Sites chart fit particular subtopics of the field trip. Adjust the subtopics and sites as necessary to suit your particular curriculum.

Please note: The following are *general* sites. Within each category you will need to select the appropriate sites to fit your particular state. Plan for a couple hours of selecting various URLs within these categories in order to meet the specific goals of your curricular unit.

Chapter 7

	Internet Sites (Sorted by Subtopic)	
Subtopic	Title of Site and URL	Notes about Site
Geography	Color Landform Atlas of the United States fermi.jhuapl.edu/states/states.html	Every map you could possibly want for your state is either on this site or linked to this site.
Cities	Yahoo!—Regional: U.S. States local.yahoo.com	Select a state. Click on the "cities" link, then select major cities in your state to visit. Select appropriate sites to visit from the following valuable links: "community," "entertainment and arts," "recreation and sports," and "travel and transportation." (Note: not all of these categories are available for smaller cities.) See ca.dir.yahoo/Regional for information specific to Canada.
History	Yahoo!—Regional: U.S. States local.yahoo.com	Select a state, then "arts and humanities," then "history." Select appropriate sites for your state and your curriculum. See ca.dir.yahoo/Regional for information specific to Canada.
Culture	Yahoo!—Regional: U.S. States local.yahoo.com	Select a state, then select appropriate sites from the following links: "arts and humanities," "community and culture," "entertainment," "recreation and sports," "science," "social science," and "travel and transportation." See ca.dir.yahoo/Regional for information specific to Canada.
Personalities	Lives, the Biography Resource amillionlives.com	Type in the names of famous people from your state and get information and pictures. Select "regions" under "collections" for information grouped by region, including some states (but not all). Select "Canadians" under "special collections" for biographies of Canadians.
Documents	Don Mabry's Historical Text Archive www.historicaltextarchive.com/links.php	Select "United States" for links to many primary documents important to almost every state. Select "Canada" for links to Canadian documents.

Graphic Organization of the Trip

The graphic organizer below demonstrates visually how the various subtopics and websites relate to the overall virtual field trip. You may want to recreate or photocopy this chart for your students before they take the trip.

Please note: You will need to select subtopics appropriate to your particular state and curriculum. The following are suggested areas to cover.

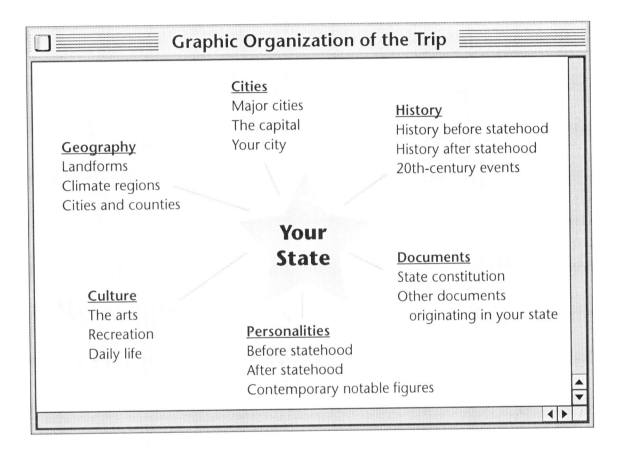

The Multiple Intelligences

The chart on the following page is a tool to help you integrate the multiple intelligences into your curricular unit. The chart provides you with a list of specific ways to use the multiple intelligences before, during, and after the virtual field trip. (See page 128 for a description of the multiple intelligences.) Please note these are teaching suggestions, not mandates. You should choose what you have time for and what is appropriate for your class. You can also use these suggestions as a springboard for additional ideas.

Using the Multiple Intelligences	
Intelligence	Activities
Verbal/ Linguistic	• Read and discuss online material. • Read aloud an important speech. • Write a speech or hold a debate about a current topic in your state. • Learn about a famous author from your state.
Logical/ Mathematical	• Explore various items and information from the trip, possibly manipulating data and materials in a final project or discussion. • Compare and contrast two major cities. • Compare and contrast two different time periods in your state.
Visual/ Spatial	• View pictures of the state. • Discuss artists of the state and view their work. • Create a collage that incorporates various facets of your state. • Recreate pictures of the state flower, bird, and so forth.
Bodily/ Kinesthetic	• Dramatically recreate a famous event in your state's history. • Learn the dances of various cultures in your state. • Impersonate a famous person from your state.
Musical/ Rhythmic	• Learn music from famous state composers. • Discuss the different venues for music in your state, such as concert halls, clubs, parks, the street, and how the music is influenced by its venue. • Listen to traditional music of various cultures in your state. • Write a new state song.
Interpersonal	• Work as a group within the unit. • Focus on different cities in small groups, then present information about each city to the class. • As a group, write a poem about the state, taking turns writing each line. • In small groups, invent a new state, including geography, climate, state song, state motto, state bird, and so forth.
Intrapersonal	• Make individual choices during personal exploration time on the virtual field trip. • Write about personal experiences in various parts of the state. • Write about personal likes and dislikes regarding the state. • Share opinions about important current events in the state.
Naturalist	• Make a timeline of events in your state's history. • Investigate the plants and animals native to your state. • Create top ten lists that classify cities according to size, natural beauty, art and entertainment offerings, and so forth.

Suggestions for Final Projects

- Using online material and graphics, create a travelogue for someone visiting your state.
- Write a research paper on the state, or some region within the state. Include sections on geography, history, important personalities, and culture.
- Create a state museum for which the students work in groups to create exhibits that illustrate different aspects of your state.

Virtual Field Trip 2: The Declaration of Independence

 **Subject:** EARLY AMERICAN HISTORY (pre-1800)

 **Topic:** *The Declaration of Independence*

 **Grade Range:** 5–11 (Adapt the material to the reading levels of your students.)

 **Primary Objective:** As a result of this virtual field trip, the students will have a better understanding of how the events, personalities, and culture of the time period affected the writing and adoption of the Declaration of Independence.

 **Subtopics:**
- Primary documents
- Important personalities connected to the signing of the document
- Historic Philadelphia
- Cultural aspects of the time
- Modern interpretations of the material

Integration into the Unit

- Focus of learning activities before the trip: introduction to the Declaration of Independence; the Acts of Parliament concerning the American colonies; the personalities most important to this event and era (such as Thomas Jefferson, Benjamin Franklin, John Adams, Abigail Adams, Betsy Ross, John Hancock, and King George III).
- Focus of learning activities after the trip: American and British responses to the Declaration; American symbols (such as the Liberty Bell, Statue of Liberty, and Uncle Sam); George Washington and the Revolutionary War.

 **Time Frame for the Trip:** 2–4 hours, depending on the age of the students and to what depth you want the class to investigate

Internet Sites

The chart on the following page groups the various "stops" on the virtual field trip by subtopic. As you plan for the virtual field trip, take the steps on page 77 to ensure a successful trip.

Internet Sites (Sorted by Subtopic)		
Subtopic	Title of Site and URL	Notes about Site
Primary Documents	The American Colonist's Library Personal.pitnet.net/primarysources	Look at the actual texts of all of the Acts of Parliament concerning the American colonies, especially the Tea, Sugar, Townshend, and Coercive Acts of 1774 (listed separately).
	The American Revolution Home Page www.dell.homestead.com/revwar/files/index.htm	This site includes images, a timeline, important documents of the era, and information about important figures. Click on "Declaration of Independence" in the timeline for background information and images, including Trumbull's painting *Signing the Declaration of Independence*. Scroll to the bottom of the main page (after you enter the site) for a link to "13 Things You Never Knew about the American Revolution."
	Don Mabry's Historical Text Archive historicaltextarchive.com/links.php	Select "United States," then "Revolution," and open *Common Sense*, by Thomas Paine.
Personalities	Lives, the Biography Resource amillionlives.com	Look up biographies of Thomas Jefferson, Benjamin Franklin, John Adams, Abigail Adams, Betsy Ross, John Hancock, and King George III.
Historic Philadelphia	A Guide to Old Covered Bridges william-king.www.drexel.edu/top/bridge/CB1.html	Look at pictures of the Pennsylvania countryside.
	Virtual Tour of Historic Philadelphia www.ushistory.org/tour/index.html	Take a virtual tour through historic Philadelphia, including Independence Hall.
	The National Park Service: Independence National Historical Park www.nps.gov/inde/exindex.htm	Look at pictures of the historic monuments.
Culture	The Food Timeline www.gti.net/mocolib1/kid/food.html	This site includes recipes from the era that you can make with your students using store-bought ingredients. Try "dried apples from Paul Revere's kitchen" and "firecakes and pepper pot from Valley Forge."
	Loyalist, British Songs and Poetry of the American Revolution users.erols.com/candidus/music.htm	Read lyrics and an explanation of the songs. Download music for some of the songs.
	1777 Colonial Paper Money www.7cs.com/colonial/1777pa.htm	View pictures of colonial paper money.
Modern Interpretations	Founding.com www.founding.com/gohome.htm	Select "The Declaration of Independence" for a discussion of the meaning of the document, including historical context, a glossary, a copy of Jefferson's rough draft, and more.
	1776—The Musical www.geocities.com/Broadway/Wing/5800	View pictures, download recordings, and read about the Broadway musical.

1. Take the trip first. Explore the various Internet sites yourself, before the students take the trip. This will give you a good idea of what material is covered, how appropriate it is for your students, and what learning adaptations you need to make, such as focusing on sites that suit your students' reading levels. You will also have the opportunity to time the trip and to check out physical aspects of the site, such as the need for plug-ins (see page 124) or extra time to download graphics.

2. Add, remove, or update sites. This is your opportunity to find alternatives if sites are unavailable. (See page 69 for information on finding alternative sites.) It is crucial for you to check the sites *before* your students begin the experience.

3. Study the chart organization. Note how the sites in the Internet Sites chart fit particular subtopics of the field trip. Adjust the subtopics and sites as necessary to suit your particular curriculum. (See also the sample web page information for this trip starting on page 44.)

Graphic Organization of the Trip

The graphic organizer below demonstrates visually how the various subtopics and websites relate to the overall virtual field trip. You may want to recreate or photocopy this chart for your students before they take the trip.

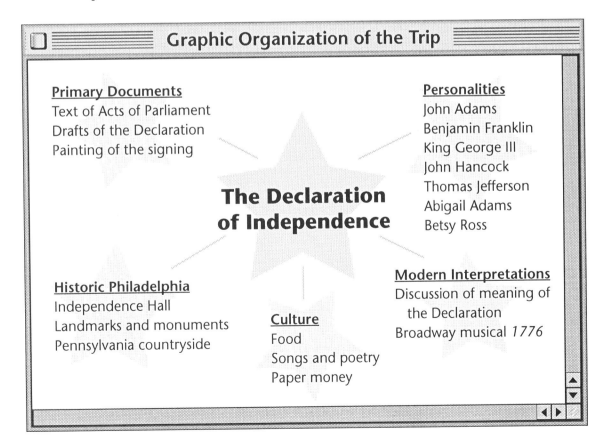

The Multiple Intelligences

The chart on the following page is a tool to help you integrate the multiple intelligences into your curricular unit. The chart provides you with a list of specific ways to use the multiple intelligences before, during, and after the virtual field trip. (See page 128 for a description of the multiple intelligences.) Please note these are teaching suggestions, not mandates. You should choose what you have time for and what is appropriate for your class. You can also use these suggestions as a springboard for additional ideas.

Suggestions for Final Projects

- Role-play as delegates to the Second Continental Congress. Each student takes a different identity and researches his background and positions on various pertinent issues.

- View the movie musical *1776* and compare information in this historical movie with material on the virtual field trip.

- Report on colonial America. Suggested topics to cover: the history of the individual colonies, the British Parlimentary acts against the colonies, the colonists' responses, personalities of the period.

- Create a "*Time* magazine" of that period. Suggested topics to cover: the history of the individual colonies, the British legislation against the colonies, the colonists' responses, personalities of the period.

Using the Multiple Intelligences

Intelligence	Activities
Verbal/ Linguistic	• Read and discuss online material. • Write a story about one the founding fathers from the perspective of a family member, such as Thomas Jefferson's wife. • Create a dictionary that defines terms and slang of the period (or just terms used in the Declaration).
Logical/ Mathematical	• Explore various items and information from the trip, possibly manipulating data and materials in a final project or discussion. • Compare and contrast the rough draft and final version of the Declaration of Independence. • Hold a debate about a key figure, such as Benjamin Franklin: Did history make the man or woman or did the man or woman make history?
Visual/ Spatial	• View images on the trip. • Draw a picture of an important event during the period. • Create a Revolutionary War map. • Create a comic strip about one of the figures or events of the period.
Bodily/ Kinesthetic	• Reenact the painting Signing the Declaration of Independence. • Try one of the recipes of the period at home or in class. • Create a walking tour (within the classroom) of historic monuments.
Musical/ Rhythmic	• Learn a Revolutionary War song. • Write a new Revolutionary War song. • Discuss the role of music in battle.
Interpersonal	• Work as a group within the unit. • Divide into two groups, one representing the British, one representing the colonists, and debate the issues of the period. • Divide into groups that focus on different aspects of the period and present each aspect to the class.
Intrapersonal	• Make individual choices during personal exploration time on the virtual field trip. • Write a diary in the voice of a person from the era, such as a founding father, a patriot or Tory soldier, an everyday colonist, or a woman running the farm while her husband is at war. • Discuss or write about what life today would be like if the Revolutionary War never happened.
Naturalist	• Make a timeline of the events leading up to the Declaration of Independence. • Discuss the role nature played in the Revolution (such as its use in battle). • Explore the differences and similarities between the natural settings of Britain and the American colonies.

Virtual Field Trip 3: The Civil War

MIDDLE AMERICAN HISTORY (1800–1900)

The Civil War

5–12 (Adapt the material to the reading levels of your students.)

As a result of this virtual field trip, the students will have a better understanding of how the events, personalities, and culture of the time affected American society during the Civil War period.

- Events of the era, including battles and historic locations
- Important documents written during this time
- Slavery during this period
- Culture of the period
- Personalities of the most important people of the period
- Personalities of everyday people of the period

Integration into the Unit

- Focus of learning activities before the trip: the background of slavery and the events that led up to the war

- Focus of learning activities after the trip: Reconstruction; Lincoln's assassination; a detailed study of the material on the trip; politics before and during the war; responses of other countries to the Civil War; various personalities the trip doesn't cover (such as Robert E. Lee)

4–8 hours, depending on the age of the students, to what depth you want the class to investigate, and whether you use all of the subtopics

Internet Sites

The chart that begins on the following page groups the various "stops" on the virtual field trip by subtopic. As you plan for the virtual field trip, take the steps on page 83 to ensure a successful trip.

Internet Sites (Sorted by Subtopic)

Subtopic	Title of Site and URL	Notes about Site
The Events of the Era	The Civil War Artillery Page www.cwartillery.org/artillery.html	Read extensive material about and view pictures of the various weapons, equipment, and other related materials used in the war.
	Civil War Battle Summaries by State www2.cr.nps.gov/abpp/battles/bystate.htm	Read data about each battle fought in the war (no pictures, but many facts).
	Hargrett Library Rare Map Collection–American Civil War scarlett.libs.uga.edu/darchive/hargrett/maps/civil.html	View dozens of authentic primary source maps produced during the war years.
	The History Place: U.S. Civil War 1861–1865 www.historyplace.com/civilwar/index.html	View and read an excellent timeline with pictures connected to important events.
	Civil War Period Uniforms and Accouterments extlab1.entnem.ufl.edu/olustee/uniforms/uniforms.html	View examples of soldiers' uniforms and equipment.
Documents	CSA Constitution sunsite.utk.edu/civil-war/csaconst.htm	View the text of the Constitution of the Confederate States of America.
	The Emancipation Proclamation www.nara.gov/exhall/featured-document/eman/emanproc.html	View transcribed text along with a reproduction of the document. Read discussion about the document and listen to an audio recording of a former slave discussing life after the Proclamation.
	The Gettysburg Address lcweb.loc.gov/exhibits/gadd	Read drafts and information about the text and the event. View a photograph of Lincoln at Gettysburg.
	Liberty Online: The Works of Lincoln libertyonline.hypermall.com/Lincoln/Default.htm	Read text of Lincoln's inaugural addresses.
Slavery	American Slave Narratives xroads.virginia.edu/~hyper/wpa/wpahome.html	Read 1930s transcripts of interviews with over 2,000 former slaves. The site includes sound files.
	Uncle Tom's Cabin and American Culture www.iath.virginia.edu/utc/sitemap.html	Read lots of background material on the causes, background, responses to, and aspects of slavery. Read or listen to songs and poems about Harriet Beecher Stowe's *Uncle Tom's Cabin*.
	The Underground Railroad @ National Geographic.com www.nationalgeographic.com/features/99/railroad/j1.html	Take a virtual field trip through the Underground Railroad, which includes pictures, sound, and a tremendous amount of information.
	United States Colored Troops in the Civil War www.coax.net/people/lwf/data.htm	Read histories and view pictures of African Americans who fought in the war.

(continued on next page)

(continued from page 81)

Internet Sites (Sorted by Subtopic)

Subtopic	Title of Site and URL	Notes about Site
Culture	The CWi Civil War Cookbook www.civilwarinteractive.com/cookbook.htm	View a complete guide to cooking in the Civil War period, with information and many recipes.
	Poetry and Music of the War between the States users.erols.com/kfraser	View lots of poetry and music examples from both the North and the South. This site is a great resource for investigating the culture of the time. (For actual recordings of these songs, visit the Civil War Music Store at bizweb.lightspeed.net/~cwms.)
	Money in the 1860s hometown.aol.com/webmasacwa/index.html	View pictures of and explore links to the various forms of money used during the period.
Famous Personalities	Civil War Biographies webpages.marshall.edu/~hughes11/biographies.htm	Read information about and view pictures of just about every major personality in the Civil War period.
	The History Place Presents Abraham Lincoln www.historyplace.com/lincoln/index.html	View an extensive timeline, photos, and text from speeches, letters, and other documents.
	Jefferson Davis Chronology www.ruf.rice.edu/~pjdavis/chron.htm	View a timeline with links to more information about the important events in Davis's life, especially during the war period.
	Ulysses S. Grant Home Page www.mscomm.com/~ulysses	Read extensive information about Grant and view photos.
	Sojourner Truth Institute www.sojournertruth.org/	Click on "history" to read Truth's biography and link to various images of people and places during the Civil War era.
Everyday People	Civil War—An Illinois Soldier www.ioweb.com/civilwar	Read the diary entries and memoirs of an ordinary soldier in the Union Army.
	TreasureNet Historical Image Collection www.treasurenet.com/images/civilwar	View hundreds of photographs covering all types of people throughout the war period. Click on pictures for a full-page image.
	Women in the Civil War userpages.aug.com/captbarb/femvets2.html	Read numerous examples of the roles women played in the war.

1. Take the trip first. Explore the various Internet sites yourself, before the students take the trip. This will give you a good idea of what material is covered, how appropriate it is for your students, and what learning adaptations you need to make, such as focusing on sites that suit your students' reading levels. You will also have the opportunity to time the trip and to check out physical aspects of the site, such as the need for plug-ins (see page 124) or extra time to download graphics.

2. Add, remove, or update sites. This is your opportunity to double-check that all of the sites are available. You may need to find alternatives. (See page 69 for information on finding alternative sites.) It is crucial for you to check the sites *before* your students begin the experience.

3. Study the chart organization. Note how the sites in the Internet Sites chart fit particular subtopics of the field trip. Adjust the subtopics and sites as necessary to suit your particular curriculum.

Graphic Organization of the Trip

The graphic organizer below demonstrates visually how the various subtopics and websites relate to the overall virtual field trip. You may want to recreate or photocopy this chart for your students before they take the trip.

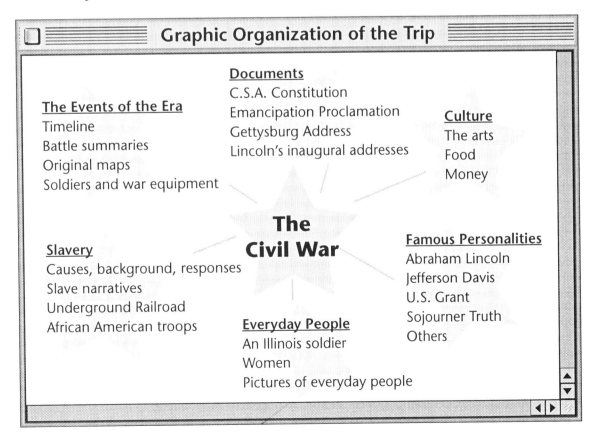

Chapter 7

The Multiple Intelligences

The chart on the following page is a tool to help you integrate the multiple intelligences into your curricular unit. The chart provides you with a list of specific ways to use the multiple intelligences before, during, and after the virtual field trip. (See page 128 for a description of the multiple intelligences.) Please note these are teaching suggestions, not mandates. You should choose what you have time for and what is appropriate for your class. You can also use these suggestions as a springboard for additional ideas.

Suggestions for Final Projects

- Role-play a peace conference for solving the Civil War crisis. Each student takes a different identity and researches the person's background and positions on various pertinent issues.
- Create a county fair of the Civil War period.
- Write a report on some aspect of the Civil War. Suggested topics to cover: battles, events (such as the Emancipation Proclamation), culture (including dress, food, music), slavery, or personalities, such as Jefferson Davis or U.S. Grant.
- Create a "*Time* magazine" of that period. Suggested topics to cover: battles, events such as Sherman's march, culture (including dress, food, music), slavery, or personalities, such as Abraham Lincoln or Harriet Beecher Stowe.
- Write a family history for a fictional family that has one son fighting for the North and one fighting for the South.

Using the Multiple Intelligences

Intelligence	Activities
Verbal/ Linguistic	• Read and discuss online material. • Perform a famous speech of the period. • Create a Civil War crossword puzzle. • Write an imaginary interview with a famous figure.
Logical/ Mathematical	• Explore various items and information from the trip, possibly manipulating data and materials in a final project or discussion. • Compare and contrast the experiences of slaves as expressed in the narratives you read or listened to on the trip. For example, compare the narratives of slaves on plantations and slaves in the city, or compare the experiences of female slaves and male slaves. • Create a "Guess Who I Am?" game using clues about famous or everyday people. • Predict what would have happened if Lincoln hadn't been assassinated or if the Civil War had not taken place when it did.
Visual/ Spatial	• View images on the trip. • Create a map showing key locations of the Civil War. • Recreate the clothing and uniforms of the day on paper figures.
Bodily/ Kinesthetic	• Reenact various aspects and events of the Civil War period. • Try one of the recipes of the period at home or in class. • Create and play a Civil War game, using a map as the game board.
Musical/ Rhythmic	• Learn a Civil War song. • Explore the importance of music in war (perhaps using Robert E. Lee's quote as a starting point: "You cannot have an army without music.") • Explore the importance of music to slaves.
Interpersonal	• Work as a group within the unit. • Divide into groups representing the North and the South and debate an important issue of the period. • Divide into small groups, with one person in a group representing a Civil War–era figure: for example, a union soldier, a confederate soldier, a famous personality, a slave, a woman. Research the life of each figure and discuss as a group.
Intrapersonal	• Make individual choices during personal exploration time on the virtual field trip. • Keep a journal of personal feelings and impressions during the field trip. • Write an "If I were Lincoln, I would . . ." essay.
Naturalist	• Make a timeline of the events of the Civil War period. • Explore the role horses played in the military. • Explore how the geographical differences between the North and South affected the Civil War.

Virtual Field Trip 4: The Great Depression

 **Subject:** MODERN AMERICAN HISTORY (1900–present)

 **Topic:** *The Great Depression*

 **Grade Range:** 5–11 (Adapt the material to the reading levels of your students.)

 **Primary Objective:** As a result of this virtual field trip, the students will have a better understanding of the events, personalities, and culture of the Great Depression era in modern American history.

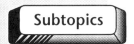 **Subtopics:**
- The daily lives of the American people during the Great Depression
- The culture of the era before and after the Great Depression
- Important personalities that had an impact on the Great Depression
- Proposed solutions to the Great Depression

Integration into the Unit

- Focus of learning activities before the trip: causes of the Great Depression; an introduction to the era
- Focus of learning activities after the trip: results of the New Deal; effects on current American culture; certain specific events (such as the Supreme Court manipulation by Roosevelt); the Great Depression around the world; responses to events in Europe preceding World War II

 **Time Frame for the Trip:** 2–4 hours, depending on the age of the students and to what depth you want the class to investigate

Internet Sites

The chart on the following page groups the various "stops" on the virtual field trip by subtopic. As you plan for the virtual field trip, take the steps on page 88 to ensure a successful trip.

Internet Sites (Sorted by Subtopic)

Subtopic	Title of Site and URL	Notes about Site
Daily Lives	America in the 1930s xroads.virginia.edu/~1930s/home_1.html	This site is a multimedia presentation of various aspects of the era: print, film, radio, and images. You will need plug-ins to make the most of this site.
	Dear Mrs. Roosevelt newdeal.feri.org/eleanor/index.htm	Read material on how the Depression affected children, including letters from children to the first lady and the personal responses of Mrs. Roosevelt.
	New Deal Network Photo Gallery newdeal.feri.org/library/index.htm	View hundreds of pictures from the Depression period, organized by category, including artwork from the era.
	We Made Do—Recalling the Great Depression www.mcsc.k12.in.us/mhs/social/madedo	Created by an Indiana high school, this site includes transcribed oral histories and photographs of life during the Depression. Includes a section where your students can add stories of their own families' experiences. Also includes a list of prices for various items in Indiana during the Depression.
Culture	Home Plate: 1930s Baseball History rampages.onramp.net/~wordwork/index.html	A history of baseball in the period, with a focus on the Beaumont Exporters. Click on "lineup" for articles and a link to selected websites with further information.
	The Jazz Age: Flapper Culture and Style www.geocities.com/flapper_culture	View pictures and read information about the culture of the 20s, leading up to the Depression.
	Screwball Comedy hamp.hampshire.edu/~pswF94/cusp/nostalgia/screw.html	Read about the role of movies in helping people get through the Depression.
Personalities	Franklin D. Roosevelt Library and Museum www.fdrlibrary.marist.edu/sitemap.html	This site contains photos, a timeline, links, and lots of information concerning F.D.R.
	Herbert Hoover Presidential Library and Museum hoover.nara.gov	View lots of information and pictures concerning Herbert Hoover. Select "just for kids" for a Hoover bio, presidential cartoons, a timeline, and more.
	Will Rogers www.ellensplace.net/rogers.html	View material and pictures on the famous humorist who helped people get through the Depression.
	The American Experience: Eleanor Roosevelt www.pbs.org/wgbh/amex/eleanor/	Read about the influential first lady, including a timeline of her life and a biography.
Solutions	Exhibit: A New Deal for the Arts www.nara.gov/exhall/newdeal/newdeal.html	Read information on how Roosevelt helped employ many people through the arts.
	Roosevelt's Fireside Chats: Outlining the New Deal Program newdeal.feri.org/chat/chat02.htm	Read the text of the fireside chat given on Sunday, May 7, 1933, outlining the New Deal to the nation.
	TVA: Electricity for All newdeal.feri.org/tva/index.htm	View a lot of information about the Tennessee Valley Authority, one of the major New Deal projects that, among other things, put many unemployed back to work.

1. Take the trip first. Explore the various Internet sites yourself, before the students take the trip. This will give you a good idea of what material is covered, how appropriate it is for your students, and what learning adaptations you need to make, such as focusing on sites that suit your students' reading levels. You will also have the opportunity to time the trip and to check out physical aspects of the site, such as the need for plug-ins (see page 124) or extra time to download graphics.

2. Add, remove, or update sites. This is your opportunity to double-check that all of the sites are available. You may need to find alternatives. (See page 69 for information on finding alternative sites.) It is crucial for you to check the sites *before* your students begin the experience.

3. Study the chart organization. Note how the sites in the Internet Sites chart fit particular subtopics of the field trip. Adjust the subtopics and sites as necessary to suit your particular curriculum.

Graphic Organization of the Trip

The graphic organizer below demonstrates visually how the various subtopics and websites relate to the overall virtual field trip. You may want to recreate or photocopy this chart for your students before they take the trip.

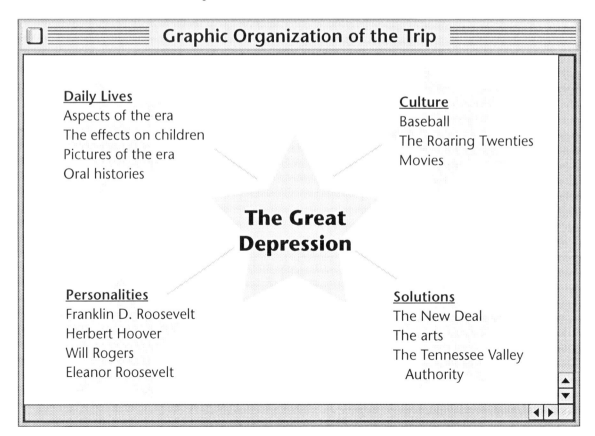

The Multiple Intelligences

The chart on the following page is a tool to help you integrate the multiple intelligences into your curricular unit. The chart provides you with a list of specific ways to use the multiple intelligences before, during, and after the virtual field trip. (See page 128 for a description of the multiple intelligences.) Please note these are teaching suggestions, not mandates. You should choose what you have time for and what is appropriate for your class. You can also use these suggestions as a springboard for additional ideas.

Suggestions for Final Projects

- Role-play as members of Congress. Each student takes a different identity and researches the person's background and positions on various pertinent issues as the class debates issues and solutions connected to the Great Depression and Roosevelt's proposals.

- Write a family history of a fictional family during the Great Depression period.

- Write a report on some aspect of the Great Depression. Suggested topics to cover: events and issues of the period (such as unemployment or the Dust Bowl), agencies created or operating during the time (such as the Tennessee Valley Authority), personalities of the era (such as Franklin or Eleanor Roosevelt or Will Rogers).

Using the Multiple Intelligences

Intelligence	Activities
Verbal/ Linguistic	• Read and discuss online material. • Write a speech modeled after Roosevelt's Fireside Chats, proposing a solution to some aspect of the Depression or addressing a current issue in the style of Roosevelt. • Read aloud the oral histories of life during the Depression. • Debate an important issue of the era.
Logical/ Mathematical	• Explore various items and information from the trip, possibly manipulating data and materials in a final project or discussion. • Compare and contrast life in the '30s with life in the '20s (or another decade). • Create a "Living and Working during the Depression" game using the average wages and prices of various items during the Depression.
Visual/ Spatial	• View images on the trip. • Draw presidential cartoons that reflect events during the presidencies of Hoover and F.D.R. • Create a timeline using only images. • Study art created during this period.
Bodily/ Kinesthetic	• Recreate events or life at this time. • Discuss the performance techniques and genres of film and theater during the Depression and how they relate to the era. • Create and play a game of charades using the people, places, things, and events of the era. • Act out plays written during this period.
Musical/ Rhythmic	• Study and sing music composed during this period. • Explore the changes in music from the '20s to the '30s. • Create a song about living during the Depression.
Interpersonal	• Work as a group within the unit. • Divide into groups, with each member of the group studying a particular subtopic in class and then teaching others about the topic. • In groups, with each group representing an important figure, create interview questions for other groups to answer about the person.
Intrapersonal	• Make individual choices during personal exploration time on the virtual field trip. • Write an essay describing what it would be like to be a child during the Depression. • Write about a Depression-era person (famous or everyday) you can relate to most.
Naturalist	• Make a timeline of the events leading up to and occurring during the Great Depression period. • Explore the experiences of farmers during the Depression, paying particular attention to the causes and effects of the Dust Bowl. • Explore the effects of the Tennessee Valley Authority on the environment.

Virtual Field Trip 5: Ancient Greece

EARLY WORLD HISTORY (B.C.E.)

Ancient Greece

5–11 (Adapt the material to the age and reading levels of your students.)

As a result of this virtual field trip, the students will have a better understanding of the culture, lifestyle, and accomplishments of ancient Greek civilization.

- Maps and famous landmarks of ancient Greece
- The daily life of the Greeks
- Arts and recreational activities of the Greeks
- Greek advancements in the sciences
- Examples of Greek literature
- Religion of the Greeks

Integration into the Unit

- Focus of learning activities before the trip: basic background of the period and of Greek culture; the stories of *The Iliad* and *The Odyssey*
- Focus of the learning activities after the trip: Greek philosophy as manifested through, and from, Greek culture; history of ancient Greece; Greek government

2–4 hours, depending on the age of the students and to what depth you want the class to investigate

Internet Sites

The chart on the following page groups the various "stops" on the virtual field trip by subtopic. As you plan for the virtual field trip, take the steps on page 93 to ensure a successful trip.

Internet Sites (Sorted by Subtopic)

Subtopic	Title of Site and URL	Notes about Site
Maps and Landmarks	Ancient Greek Cities www.sikyon.com/index.html	This site contains information, pictures, and links to more detailed information.
	OSSHE Historical and Cultural Atlas Resource—Europe: darkwing.uoregon.edu/~atlas/europe	Select from a variety of maps from different times during this age.
	Museums, Monuments, and Archaeological Sites of Hellas www.culture.gr/2/21/toc/index.html	View pictures and information on every possible important ancient site. Click on pictures for a larger image.
Daily Life	The Ancient Greek World www.museum.upenn.edu/Greek_World/Intro.html	Look at special sections with pictures and information concerning land and time, daily life, economy, religion, and death.
	British Museum Ancient Greeks Virtual Tour atschool.eduweb.co.uk/allsouls/bm/ag1.html	From the British Museum, this site contains pictures of actual artifacts from everyday life, with information about the artifacts. Select the "map of the ground floor tour" or a tour of "room 69."
Arts and Recreation	Ancient Greek Theater users.groovy.gr/~ekar/index.html	Learn everything you would want to know about Greek theater. View lots of information and pictures.
	Looking at Art of Ancient Greece and Rome: An Online Exhibition www.artsednet.getty.edu/ArtsEdNet/Resources/Beauty/index.html	View selections from the famous J. Paul Getty Museum in Los Angeles. This site also includes information about the art and suggestions for student activities.
	Olympics through Time www.fhw.gr/projects/olympics/	View information and pictures concerning the early Greek Olympic period.
The Sciences	Antiqua Medicina: From Homer to Vesalius www.med.virginia.edu/hs-library/historical/antiqua/anthome.html	This site goes through the early developments in medicine, providing lots of information, stories, and quotations from famous Greeks.
	Ships of the Ancient Greeks www.bulfinch.org/fables/grkship.html	View pictures and drawings of various types of Greek ships, as well as information about the ships and the Greek navy.
Literature	The Classics Pages www.users.globalnet.co.uk/~loxias/oldindex.htm	This site is a lot of interactive fun: Students role-play and learn about aspects of the most important Greek writings and mythology.
	Homer's *Iliad* and *Odyssey* library.thinkquest.org/19300/data/homer.htm	Read in-depth background material created by students on these two Greek classics, including text of the classics themselves.
Religion	The Encyclopedia Mythica www.pantheon.org/mythica.html	Find brief information on virtually every god ever worshiped throughout pagan history.

1. Take the trip first. Explore the various Internet sites yourself, before the students take the trip. This will give you a good idea of what material is covered, how appropriate it is for your students, and what learning adaptations you need to make, such as focusing on sites that suit your students' reading levels. You will also have the opportunity to time the trip and to check out physical aspects of the site, such as the need for plug-ins (see page 124) or extra time to download graphics.

2. Add, remove, or update sites. This is your opportunity to double-check that all of the sites are available. You may need to find alternatives. (See page 69 for information on finding alternative sites.) It is crucial for you to check the sites *before* your students begin the experience.

3. Study the chart organization. Note how the sites in the Internet Sites chart fit particular subtopics of the field trip. Adjust the subtopics and sites as necessary to suit your particular curriculum.

Graphic Organization of the Trip

The graphic organizer below demonstrates visually how the various subtopics and websites relate to the overall virtual field trip. You may want to recreate or photocopy this chart for your students before they take the trip.

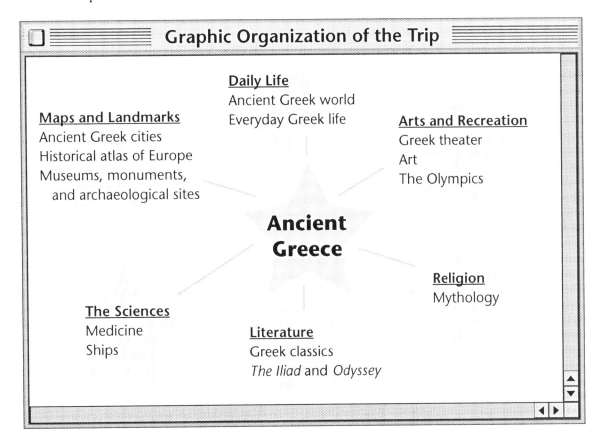

The Multiple Intelligences

The chart on the following page is a tool to help you integrate the multiple intelligences into your curricular unit. The chart provides you with a list of specific ways to use the multiple intelligences before, during, and after the virtual field trip. (See page 128 for a description of the multiple intelligences.) Please note these are teaching suggestions, not mandates. You should choose what you have time for and what is appropriate for your class. You can also use these suggestions as a springboard for additional ideas.

Suggestions for Final Projects

- Recreate a day at the agora (Greek marketplace), with booths representing various aspects of ancient Greek culture.

- Write a report on ancient Greece. Suggested topics: events and issues of the time, mythology, aspects of culture, famous personalities.

- Role-play a debate between the gods and humans concerning the role of gods in everyday life.

Using the Multiple Intelligences	
Intelligence	Activities
Verbal/ Linguistic	• Read and discuss online material. • Write a new myth, inventing new gods, new heroes, and so forth. • Compare and contrast the role of writers in ancient Greece with writers today, including how society views them. • Read an example of Greek literature.
Logical/ Mathematical	• Explore various items and information from the trip, possibly manipulating data and materials in a final project or discussion. • Study examples of Greek mathematical concepts. • Compare and contrast ancient Greek philosophies. • Create a "Guess Who I Am" game about ancient Greek personalities.
Visual/ Spatial	• View images on the trip. • Study Greek art. • Create sculptures from clay in Greek style. • Discuss the function of art in ancient Greece. • Draw the important figures in Greek mythology.
Bodily/ Kinesthetic	• Recreate events in Greek culture, including mythology. • Act out a Greek play. • Explore the importance of the Olympics in ancient Greece. • Create a new Olympic event and discuss how the Greeks might have reacted to it. • Build a model of an ancient Greek ship.
Musical/ Rhythmic	• Investigate, create, and play an instrument used in classical Greece. • Study the role of music in Greek culture. • Write a song about a myth.
Interpersonal	• Work as a group within the unit. • Study particular Greek gods and take turns impersonating each god in a class group. • In small groups, create quizzes for other groups to take.
Intrapersonal	• Make individual choices during personal exploration time on the virtual field trip. • Write a "Day in the Life" journal of an everyday citizen of ancient Greece. • Compare personal philosophy with that of an ancient Greek philosopher.
Naturalist	• Make a timeline of the events during the ancient Greek period. • Explore the role animals played (such as in chariot races) in ancient Greek culture. • Explore the role climate and geography played in shaping Greek culture.

Chapter 7

Virtual Field Trip 6: The Crusades

 **Subject** MIDDLE WORLD HISTORY (0–1700 C.E.)

 **Topic** *The Crusades*

 **Grade Range** 7–12 (Adapt the material to the age and reading levels of your students.)

 **Primary Objective** As a result of this virtual field trip, the students will have a better understanding of the period of the Crusades, including important personalities and events, along with the culture of the time.

 **Subtopics**
- Important events of the Crusades
- A geographic and pictorial outlook of where the events of the Crusades occurred
- Personalities and personal accounts of the Crusades
- Cultural aspects at the time of the Crusades

Integration into the Unit

- Focus of learning activities before the trip: basic history and philosophy of the period; goals of the Christians and Muslims

- Focus of learning activities after the trip: historical aftermath of the Crusades in Europe and the Middle East; King Arthur and other legends; religion; various famous personalities

 **Time Frame for the Trip** 2–6 hours, depending on the age of the students and to what depth you want the class to investigate

Internet Sites

The chart on the following page groups the various "stops" on the virtual field trip by subtopic. As you plan for the virtual field trip, take the steps on page 98 to ensure a successful trip.

Internet Sites (Sorted by Subtopic)

Subtopic	Title of Site and URL	Notes about Site
Events	Catholic Encyclopedia: Crusades www.newadvent.org/cathen/04543c.htm	Excellent material on this site explains every possible aspect of the Crusades, with links to further information. This is a Catholic Church site, so be aware of bias.
	The Crusades and the Contributions of Islam www.mrdowling.com/606islam.html	This site also contains excellent material on the Crusades, from the Muslim point of view. Again, be aware of bias.
Geography	Crusades: A View from Jordan www.acsamman.edu.jo/~ms/crusades	Take a tour of the ruins of crusaders' castles left behind in the country of Jordan.
	The Holy Land of the Crusaders 198.62.75.1/www1/ofm/crus/CRUmain.html	View dozens of pictures of where the crusaders went in Israel, along with pictures of their churches, symbols, castles, and locations in Europe. Click on a picture for a larger image.
	Internet Medieval Sourcebook: Maps and Images www.fordham.edu/halsall/sbookmap.html	Scroll down to the section on the Crusades for a variety of historical maps.
Personalities and Accounts	The European Middle Ages www.wsu.edu/~dee/MA/CONTENTS.HTM	Read text on the various peoples of Europe during the Middle Ages.
	Medieval Sourcebook: Soloman Bar Samson www.fordham.edu/halsall/source/1096jews-mainz.html	Read a firsthand account of the Crusades by a Jewish leader in a European village whose residents were massacred.
	Medieval Sourcebook: William of Tyre www.fordham.edu/halsall/source/tyre-cde.html	Read excerpts from a firsthand account of the Second Crusade by a Christian leader.
	Medieval Women mw.mcmaster.ca/home.html	Explore this interactive site full of pictures and information about the lives of medieval women.
Culture	Collection: Medieval and Anglo-Saxon Recipes www.cs.cmu.edu/People/mjw/recipes/ethnic/historical/med-anglosaxon-coll.html	View authentic recipes. Some are easy to make using everyday ingredients.
	English through the Ages www.bluerider.com/english	Take a brief tour of the Old and Middle English dialects.
	V@le: Cosmeston Medieval Village www.valeofglamorgan.gov.uk/cosmeston/medvill.html	Although commercial, this site has great pictures and explanations of a medieval village. Look around, especially at the "Vale scenes" link.
	Medieval Art and Architecture www1.pitt.edu/~medart/index.html	View numerous pictures and examples with explanations. Click on parts of the images for a closer look at that part.
	Medieval and Renaissance Instruments www.s-hamilton.k12.ia.us/antiqua/instrumt.html	View pictures and information on a variety of instruments. Click on a picture to hear the instrument.

1. Take the trip first. Explore the various Internet sites yourself, before the students take the trip. This will give you a good idea of what material is covered, how appropriate it is for your students, and what learning adaptations you need to make, such as focusing on sites that suit your students' reading levels. You will also have the opportunity to time the trip and to check out physical aspects of the site, such as the need for plug-ins (see page 124) or extra time to download graphics.

2. Add, remove, or update sites. This is your opportunity to double-check that all of the sites are available. You may need to find alternatives. (See page 69 for information on finding alternative sites.) It is crucial for you to check the sites *before* your students begin the experience.

3. Study the chart organization. Note how the sites in the Internet Sites chart fit particular subtopics of the field trip. Adjust the subtopics and sites as necessary to suit your particular curriculum.

Graphic Organization of the Trip

The graphic organizer below demonstrates visually how the various subtopics and websites relate to the overall virtual field trip. You may want to recreate or photocopy this chart for your students before they take the trip.

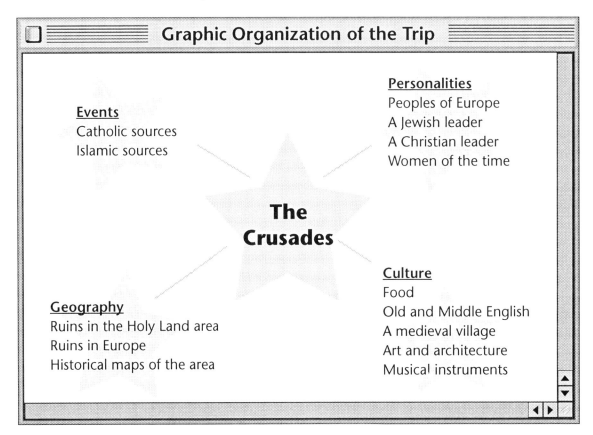

The Multiple Intelligences

The chart on the following page is a tool to help you integrate the multiple intelligences into your curricular unit. The chart provides you with a list of specific ways to use the multiple intelligences before, during, and after the virtual field trip. (See page 128 for a description of the multiple intelligences.) Please note these are teaching suggestions, not mandates. You should choose what you have time for and what is appropriate for your class. You can also use these suggestions as a springboard for additional ideas.

Suggestions for Final Projects

- Create a country faire demonstrating aspects of the culture or the time period.

- Write a report on the period of the Crusades. Suggested topics: events in Europe and the Middle East, religion, personalities.

- Write a news report or history of an event from three different perspectives: Christian, Muslim, and Jewish.

Chapter 7

\multicolumn{2}{c}{**Using the Multiple Intelligences**}	
Intelligence	Activities
Verbal/ Linguistic	• Read and discuss online material. • Read aloud firsthand accounts of the Crusades. • Create an Old English or Middle English dictionary.
Logical/ Mathematical	• Explore various items and information from the trip, possibly manipulating data and materials in a final project or discussion. • Compare and contrast two perspectives on the Crusades. • Explore current events that resemble crusades.
Visual/ Spatial	• View images on the trip. • Study art produced during this period. • Explore the function and symbolic aspects of medieval architecture. • Create a pictorial map of the Crusades using images of ruins and other important places. • Create a recruitment poster for crusaders.
Bodily/ Kinesthetic	• Reenact scenarios of the period (such as crusaders on a journey). • Try a medieval recipe. • Create a Crusades game, using a map as a gameboard.
Musical/ Rhythmic	• Create and play instruments of this time. • Explore the role of music in religion. • Write a song that incorporates key events of the Crusades.
Interpersonal	• Work as a group within the unit. • Divide into groups, with each group representing peoples involved in the Crusades. Debate or discuss the different perspectives. • Interview a personality of the era in pairs, with one person impersonating the personality and the other conducting the interview.
Intrapersonal	• Make individual choices during personal exploration time on the virtual field trip. • Keep a journal of feelings and impressions throughout the field trip. • Write a diary from the perspective of a medieval person.
Naturalist	• Make a timeline of the events associated with the Crusades period. • Discuss the importance of place in the Crusades. • Compare and contrast cities and rural areas during medieval times.

Virtual Field Trip 7: The French Revolution

 **Subject** MODERN WORLD HISTORY (1700–present)

 **Topic** *The French Revolution*

 **Grade Range** 7–12 (Adapt the material to the age and reading levels of your students.)

 **Primary Objective** As a result of this virtual field trip, the students will have a better understanding of the period of the French Revolution, including important personalities and events, along with the culture of the time.

 **Subtopics**
- The important events of the period, seen through both French and foreign eyes
- Geography and historic landmarks from the period
- Important personalities of the period
- Important documents of the period
- The culture of the era

Integration into the Unit

- Focus of learning activities before the trip: background leading up to the French Revolution
- Focus of learning activities after the trip: aftermath of the French Revolution; influence of the American Revolution on the French; influence of the church on the French

 **Time Frame for the Trip** 2–6 hours, depending on the age of the students, to what depth you want the class to investigate, and whether you use all of the subtopics

Internet Sites

The chart on the following page groups the various "stops" on the virtual field trip by subtopic. As you plan for the virtual field trip, take the steps on page 104 to ensure a successful trip.

\multicolumn{3}{c}{**Internet Sites** (Sorted by Subtopic)}
Subtopic	Title of Site and URL	Notes about Site
Events	British Newspaper Coverage of the French Revolution www.english.ucsb.edu/faculty/ayliu/research/around-1800/FR	Read about the major events of the revolution as seen by the *London Times* and *Morning Chronicle*.
	The French Revolution members.aol.com/agentmess/frenchrev/summary.html	This site provides a comprehensive summary of the various aspects and events of the period.
	The Guillotine Headquarters www.metaphor.dk/guillotine/Pages/Headquarters.html	At this site you'll find everything you would want to know about the guillotine and its use, including pictures and history.
Geography and Landmarks	Webmuseum: Paris: Tours www.ibiblio.org/wm/paris	Take a virtual tour with lots of information on modern and historical Paris, including national monuments. Select "historical guided tour." Click on pictures for full-screen images.
Personalities	Marie Antoinette Gallery www.batguano.com/VigeeMAgallery.html	View a history of Marie Antoinette with various portraits.
	Napoleon www.napoleon.org/home_us.html	This site covers everything you would want to know about Napoleon and his role in this historic period. In addition to "documentation," "information," and "museum," select "fun stuff" for a downloadable music score, online puzzles using art featuring Napoleon, an interactive map, and more.
	Portrait Gallery www.lib.utexas.edu/photodraw/portraits/index.html	View portraits (no information, however) of every major figure in the period and beyond.
Documents	Declaration of the Rights of Man and of the Citizen members.aol.com/agentmess/frenchrev/mancitizen.html	Read a copy of the Declaration.
	Declaration of the Rights of Woman and Citizen members.aol.com/agentmess/frenchrev/wmanright.html	Read a copy of the Declaration.
	Internet Modern History Sourcebook: French Revolution www.fordham.edu/halsall/mod/modsbook13.html	This site contains links to dozens of primary documents, including letters and speeches, in the following areas: The French Revolution (events leading up to, liberal revolution, radical revolution), responses to revolution, Napoleon, Napoleonic Wars.

(continued on next page)

(continued from page 102)

Internet Sites (Sorted by Subtopic)

Subtopic	Title of Site and URL	Notes about Site
Culture	**Museums of Paris** www.paris.org/Musees	View pictures from Paris museums, including the Louvre.
	18th Century Costume Resources Online www.costumes.org/pages/18thlinks.htm	Examples of the styles of dress of the French Revolution period. Select from numerous links to examples of French fashion. Scroll down for more information on the 18th century in general, including art and history.
	Cité de la Musique www.cite-musique.fr/anglais/musee/visite/18eme/index.htm	Explore pictures, information, and sound files on 18th-century French music.
	Modern History Sourcebook: Salon Life www.fordham.edu/halsall/mod/18salons.html	Read short excerpts from various memoirs concerning life in the Enlightenment, particularly within the salons held by high society women.

1. Take the trip first. Explore the various Internet sites yourself, before the students take the trip. This will give you a good idea of what material is covered, how appropriate it is for your students, and what learning adaptations you need to make, such as focusing on sites that suit your students' reading levels. You will also have the opportunity to time the trip and to check out physical aspects of the site, such as the need for plug-ins (see page 124) or extra time to download graphics.

2. Add, remove, or update sites. This is your opportunity to double-check that all of the sites are available. You may need to find alternatives. (See page 69 for information on finding alternative sites.) It is crucial for you to check the sites *before* your students begin the experience.

3. Study the chart organization. Note how the sites in the Internet Sites chart fit particular subtopics of the field trip. Adjust the subtopics and sites as necessary to suit your particular curriculum.

Graphic Organization of the Trip

The graphic organizer below demonstrates visually how the various subtopics and websites relate to the overall virtual field trip. You may want to recreate or photocopy this chart for your students before they take the trip.

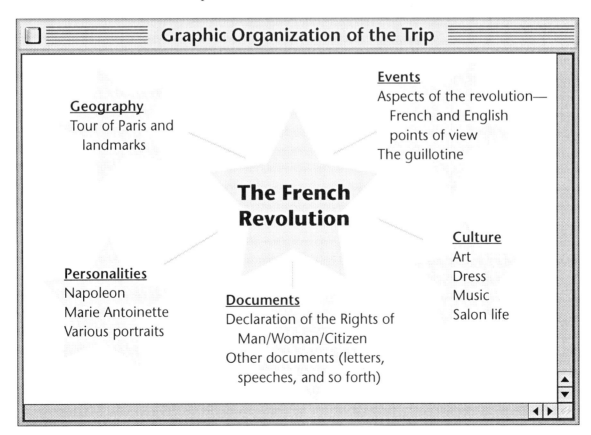

The Multiple Intelligences

The chart on the following page is a tool to help you integrate the multiple intelligences into your curricular unit. The chart provides you with a list of specific ways to use the multiple intelligences before, during, and after the virtual field trip. (See page 128 for a description of the multiple intelligences.) Please note these are teaching suggestions, not mandates. You should choose what you have time for and what is appropriate for your class. You can also use these suggestions as a springboard for additional ideas.

Suggestions for Final Projects

- Create a French or Paris "faire," demonstrating aspects of the culture and the time period. Be sure to note the differences between the rich and the common people.

- Role-play as representatives of the U.S. Congress. Each student takes a different identity and researches the person's background and positions on various pertinent issues—pro- or anti-France. Debate whether the United States should support the French Revolution.

- View a movie version of the book *Les Miserables* and compare information in this historical movie with material students discover on their virtual field trip.

- Use the material discovered on the virtual field trip to create a "*Time* magazine" of that period. Suggested topics to cover: the history of the French Revolution, culture of the time (such as the salons), and personalities of the period, such as Napoleon or Marie Antoinette.

Chapter 7

Using the Multiple Intelligences

Intelligence	Activities
Verbal/ Linguistic	• Read and discuss online material. • Write newspaper articles about the French Revolution from a French perspective and a foreign perspective (British or American). • Create a glossary of important terms during the era.
Logical/ Mathematical	• Explore various items and information from the trip, possibly manipulating data and materials in a final project or discussion. • Compare and contrast the Declaration of the Rights of Man and of the Citizen with the Declaration of the Rights of Woman and Citizen. • Compare and contrast the French Revolution with the American Revolution.
Visual/ Spatial	• View images on the trip. • Study art produced during this period. • Create a series of portraits of Napoleon, depicting him at different stages of life. • Create a Napoleon or Marie Antoinette comic strip.
Bodily/ Kinesthetic	• Reenact scenarios of the period. • Act out plays produced during this period. • Plan an 18th-century fashion show, using styles that illustrate differing social classes.
Musical/ Rhythmic	• Study and sing or play music composed during this period. • Write a song about the French Revolution. • Explore music written about the French Revolution. • Compare a piece of classical music written in France during the 18th century with a piece written in another country during the same period.
Interpersonal	• Work as a group within the unit. • In groups, recreate a French salon. • Create a walking tour of historic landmarks. Divide into small groups. Each creates a landmark using art or recorded or written information for display.
Intrapersonal	• Make individual choices during personal exploration time on the virtual field trip. • Write an "If I were . . ." essay about an important figure of the era. • Reflect on how the world would have been different in the 19th century if the French Revolution had not occurred when it did.
Naturalist	• Make a timeline of the events associated with the French Revolution. • Compare and contrast the natural setting of the French Revolution with that of the American Revolution, including how setting may have influenced the events of each war. • Explore the effect of nature on social status during this era, such as where and how people lived in the country versus the city.

Humanities Field Trips

In This Chapter

- Ways to Adapt the Virtual Field Trips (p. 108)
- Virtual Field Trip 1: Democracy (p. 110)
- Virtual Field Trip 2: The Homeless (p. 115)

Search Engines · **Directories** · **Bookmarks** · **Internet** · **Cybertrips** · **Browsers**

Chapter 8

This chapter focuses on the curricula generally taught in secondary grades. The virtual field trips in this chapter include the following topics:

- Democracy (concept course)
- The Homeless (social action)

The most important point of concern is the academic level of your students. For example, the material in the humanities can be found not only in separate high school courses, but also throughout the curriculum starting in sixth grade. Although the Internet sites on the virtual field trip are general in nature, you may need to adapt the material to the reading level and sophistication of your students. Take care not to use Internet sites that are either too difficult or too easy. (See Overview of a Virtual Field Trip, starting on page 39, for details on the field trip format.)

Ways to Adapt the Virtual Field Trips

You can substitute different subtopics in any of the field trips to match other goals in your curriculum:

- Choose a different humanities topic, concentrating on important personalities involved and their work or positions, and how the material fits into American culture, both in the past and in today's society.
- Choose another social action issue, keeping three aspects in mind: data, what others are doing, what the students can do.

Finding Additional Information

The websites and search engines in the chart on the following page are good starting points for finding additional information and sites on democracy and social issues:

Humanities Topics and Sites

Don Mabry's Historical Text Archive
www.historicaltextarchive.com/links.php
Select "United States," then the appropriate area.

History/Social Studies Website for K–12 Teachers
www.execpc.com/~dboals/boals.html
- Select "government," then appropriate subtopics.
- Locate material on other issues by selecting "religion/ethics/philosophy," then "ethics/ethical issues." Select the subtopic that best fits your issues.

The Center for Voting and Democracy
www.fairvote.org/
This site includes material on democracy with an emphasis on elections. See "web links" for more sites that explore various aspects of democracy.

Metacrawler
www.metacrawler.com
Type in a topic for the search. Select "phrase" for topics of two or more words.

Yahoo!
www.yahoo.com
- Select "government," then "U.S. government," and choose the relevant subtopics.
- Select "society and culture," then "issues and causes," then "housing," under which you'll find "homelessness." For other social issues, explore the "issues and causes" list.

Chapter 8

Virtual Field Trip 1: Democracy

 ## CONCEPT COURSES

 ### *Democracy*

 8–12 (Adapt the material to the reading levels of your students.)

 As a result of this virtual field trip, the students will have a better understanding of the concept of democracy and how it manifests itself in the United States government and culture.

- The structure of the U.S. government
- Current members of U.S. Congress
- The various political parties and their platforms and positions
- Democracy as exemplified in our culture
- Symbols of democracy, including documents and institutions

Integration into the Unit

- Focus of learning activities before the trip: a basic knowledge of the structure and workings of the American government; a basic knowledge of the Constitution and the Declaration of Independence

- Focus of learning activities after the trip: in-depth discussion of individual issues; the structures and operations of state and local governments

 4–8 hours, depending on the age and sophistication of the students and to what depth you want the class to investigate

Internet Sites

The chart on the following page groups the various "stops" on the virtual field trip by subtopic. As you plan for the virtual field trip, take the steps on page 112 to ensure a successful trip.

Internet Sites (Sorted by Subtopic)

Subtopic	Title of Site and URL	Notes about Site
The American Government	An Outline of American Government usinfo.state.gov/usa/infousa/politics/govworks/oagtoc.htm	This site includes sources and information about the rights, duties, and responsibilities of each part of the American government, including some primary source documents.
Current Politicians	United States House of Representatives www.house.gov	This home page of the House includes comprehensive information concerning the agenda, bills, roll call votes, and issues, along with representatives' e-mail addresses.
	United States Senate www.senate.gov	This home page of the Senate includes comprehensive information concerning the agenda, bills, roll call votes, and issues, along with senators' e-mail addresses. The site also displays pieces from the Senate's art collection.
The Political Parties and Their Platforms	Homework Center—Social Issues www.multnomah.lib.or.us/lib/homework/sochc.html	View information and links to information on major political issues.
	U.S.A.—Political Parties & Youth Organizations home.luna.nl/~benne/pp/nam/us/index.htm	Select from links to the websites of every imaginable political party.
	Democracy Net www.dnet.org	Read material on candidates and issues from around the country and also by individual state.
Democracy in Our Culture	About Political Humor politicalhumor.about.com	This site includes every type of political humor. Be sure to personally inspect individual sites—some are off-color and inappropriate for students.
	Webster's World of Cultural Democracy www.wwcd.org	Read information about cultural democracy, including definitions of cultural policy and cultural action, and discussion of cultural issues in democracy.
Symbols of Democracy	The Great Seal of the United States www.greatseal.com	View information about, history of, and pictures of the Great Seal.
	Don Mabry's Historical Text Archive www.historicaltextarchive.com/links.php	View copies of every important document in American history. Select "United States" and explore the relevant subtopics.
	Yahoo!: Washington, D.C.: Buildings and Monuments dir.yahoo.com/Regional/U_S__States/	Click on "Washington D.C.," then "Entertainment & Arts," then "architecture," then "buildings and monuments." View a list of websites for all the major buildings and monuments in the nation's capital.

1. Take the trip first. Explore the various Internet sites yourself, before the students take the trip. This will give you a good idea of what material is covered, how appropriate it is for your students, and what learning adaptations you need to make, such as focusing on sites that suit your students' reading levels. You will also have the opportunity to time the trip and to check out physical aspects of the site, such as the need for plug-ins (see page 124) or extra time to download graphics.

2. Add, remove, or update sites. This is your opportunity to double-check that all of the sites are available. You may need to find alternatives. (See page 109 for information on finding alternative sites.) It is crucial for you to check the sites *before* your students begin the experience.

3. Study the chart organization. Note how the sites in the Internet Sites chart fit particular subtopics of the field trip. Adjust the subtopics and sites as necessary to suit your particular curriculum.

Graphic Organization of the Trip

The graphic organizer below demonstrates visually how the various subtopics and websites relate to the overall virtual field trip. You may want to recreate or photocopy this chart for your students before they take the trip.

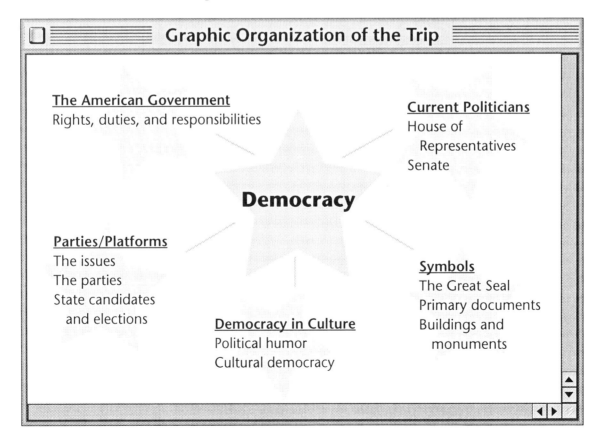

The Multiple Intelligences

The chart on the following page is a tool to help you integrate the multiple intelligences into your curricular unit. The chart provides you with a list of specific ways to use the multiple intelligences before, during, and after the virtual field trip. (See page 128 for a description of the multiple intelligences.) Please note these are teaching suggestions, not mandates. You should choose what you have time for and what is appropriate for your class. You can also use these suggestions as a springboard for additional ideas.

Suggestions for Final Projects

- Write a classroom constitution, including the rights and responsibilities of everyone involved with the classroom: students, teacher, administrators, and parents.
- Write a report on one of the issues, concentrating on a definition of the issue, varying positions people have taken on the topic, and your personal feelings based on your research.
- Hold a debate on one of the issues, or on whether we have a democracy in the United States.
- Get involved with an issue, either by volunteering time or writing to those responsible.
- Start or get involved with student government at school.

\multicolumn{2}{c}{**Using the Multiple Intelligences**}
Intelligence	Activities
Verbal/ Linguistic	• Read and discuss online material. • Write and present a speech on a current event or issue related to the mechanics of democracy, such as the Florida vote-count debate of the 2000 presidential election. • Write to your senator, representative, or the president about a current issue.
Logical/ Mathematical	• Explore various items and information from the trip, possibly manipulating data and materials in a final project or discussion. • Compare and contrast democracy in 1776 with democracy today, concentrating on the rights of various groups: ethnic, racial, religious, and gender. • Analyze an election campaign, including the issues, the debates, the speeches, the financing, the constituency, and so forth, determining the reasons behind who won and who lost.
Visual/ Spatial	• View images on the trip. • Create a detailed graphic organization that explains the structure and relationships of government, including relevant names and other details. • Draw political cartoons or a comic strip about a current event or political figure. • Construct political posters promoting democracy or some other issue.
Bodily/ Kinesthetic	• Reenact scenes exemplifying issues involving the Bill of Rights. • Create a physical game that illustrates how a bill becomes a law. • Create a new Great Seal (of any materials) that reflects modern American society.
Musical/ Rhythmic	• Learn folk songs that are about democracy, having a voice in government, and various related issues. • Write a song on a current issue. • Explore the role of music in political activism today and in past centuries.
Interpersonal	• Work as a group within the unit. • Form lobbying groups around various current issues. • Divide into groups to explore each branch of government in more depth, then present information to other groups.
Intrapersonal	• Make individual choices during personal exploration time on the virtual field trip. • Write about what you'd like to see added to the Bill of Rights. • Explore in-depth (in writing or discussion) a current issue of great importance to you.
Naturalist	• Make a timeline of the development of democracy—address the changing definition of "All men are created equal" from 1776 through today. • Examine how our government addresses environmental issues. • Use scientific classification to organize the government. For example, senators and representatives might be of the same genus (Congress), but a different species.

Virtual Field Trip 2: The Homeless

CONCEPT COURSES

The Homeless

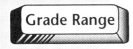

7–12 (Adapt the material to the reading and sophistication levels of your students.)

As a result of this virtual field trip, the students will have a better understanding of the situation of the homeless in the United States, what people and government are doing to help the homeless, and a working knowledge of how students can become personally involved in social action.

- The people: who is homeless (children and adults), why they are homeless, what their daily life is like
- Ways various organizations are working to alleviate the situation
- Ways that students can become involved

Integration into the Unit

- Focus of learning activities before the trip: introduction to the plight of the homeless; personal accounts (similar to those introduced on *Comic Relief*)

- Focus of learning activities after the trip: a classroom or student social-action project; local activities or situations in the students' hometown

3–6 hours, depending on the age and sophistication of the students and to what depth you want the class to investigate

Internet Sites

The chart on the following page groups the various "stops" on the virtual field trip by subtopic. As you plan for the virtual field trip, take the steps on page 117 to ensure a successful trip.

Chapter 8

Internet Sites (Sorted by Subtopic)		
Subtopic	Title of Site and URL	Notes about Site
Homeless People	How to Be Homeless: A Survivor's Guide to Living on the Streets www.newsport.sfsu.edu/s99/homeless	This site presents the different things homeless people do to get through the day.
	Play Hobson's Choice www.realchangenews.org/hobson_intro.html	Play an online simulation game that helps students imagine the situation of those in poverty and need.
	Becoming Homeless www.nationalhomeless.org/sjoblom1.html	Read the continuing story of one family's battle with homelessness.
	National Coalition for the Homeless www.nationalhomeless.org	View a tremendous amount of information on the problem of the homeless in America.
	Education of Homeless Children and Youth nch.ari.net/edchild.html	View an extensive fact sheet on homeless children.
People Trying to Help	U.S. Department of Housing and Urban Development: Homelessness www.hud.gov/homeless/index.cfm	This site includes information on federal programs for the homeless.
	Kidsacks www.ddc.com/kidsacks	Read about a program to help the homeless that involves making and providing sleeping bags for homeless children.
	Project Act www.projectact.com	Read about a school system project to benefit homeless children. Be sure to check out the shelter art exhibition.
	Real Change News www.realchangenews.org/issue/current/index.html	This is a newspaper site that features articles about solutions to poverty and homelessness. The site also includes writing and poetry by homeless writers.
	Streetwise www.streetwise.org	This independent newspaper is sold by the homeless, formerly homeless, and economically disadvantaged men and women.
Becoming Involved	54 Ways You Can Help the Homeless www.earthsystems.org/ways	This entire book is online and available for free download. It includes material on dozens of everyday ways students and adults can help the homeless problem. Scroll to the bottom for a link to a list that summarizes the 54 ways.
	The Hunger Site www.thehungersite.com	Click on the link to "donate free food" and the site's sponsors will provide a cup of food to those in need around the world. Select "about hunger" for more information on hunger around the world.
	Volunteer Match www.volunteermatch.org	Use this site to locate projects in your area. You can search by mileage from your school and types of projects with which you want to get involved.

1. Take the trip first. Explore the various Internet sites yourself, before the students take the trip. This will give you a good idea of what material is covered, how appropriate it is for your students, and what learning adaptations you need to make, such as focusing on sites that suit your students' reading levels. You will also have the opportunity to time the trip and to check out physical aspects of the site, such as the need for plug-ins (see page 124) or extra time to download graphics.

2. Add, remove, or update sites. This is your opportunity to double-check that all of the sites are available. You may need to find alternatives. (See page 109 for information on finding alternative sites.) It is crucial for you to check the sites *before* your students begin the experience.

3. Study the chart organization. Note how the sites in the Internet Sites chart fit particular subtopics of the field trip. Adjust the subtopics and sites as necessary to suit your particular curriculum.

Graphic Organization of the Trip

The graphic organizer below demonstrates visually how the various subtopics and websites relate to the overall virtual field trip. You may want to recreate or photocopy this chart for your students before they take the trip.

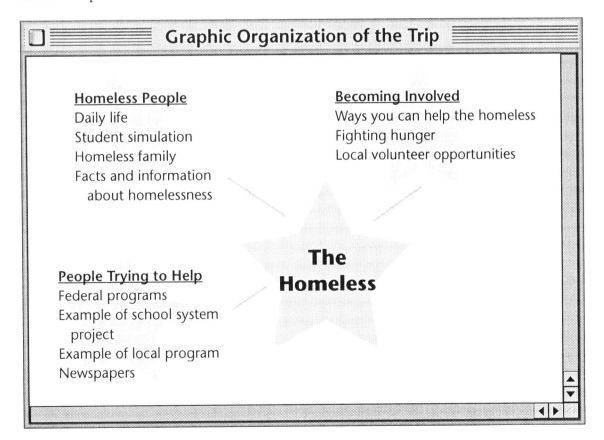

The Multiple Intelligences

The following chart is a tool to help you integrate the multiple intelligences into your curricular unit. The chart provides you with a list of specific ways to use the multiple intelligences before, during, and after the virtual field trip. (See page 128 for a description of the multiple intelligences.) Please note these are teaching suggestions, not mandates. You should choose what you have time for and what is appropriate for your class. You can also use these suggestions as a springboard for additional ideas.

Suggestions for Final Projects

- Create a schoolwide program for improving the plight of the homeless in your community.
- Use the Volunteer Match Internet site (page 116) to locate projects in your community.
- Create a "We Can Help the Homeless" pamphlet for your school, including information and projects for social action in your community.

Humanities Field Trips

Using the Multiple Intelligences

Intelligence	Activities
Verbal/ Linguistic	• Read and discuss online material. • Write a story about a homeless person. • Present a persuasive speech to encourage others to help the homeless. • Write a letter to your congressperson asking him or her to help with the plight of the homeless. Be persuasive.
Logical/ Mathematical	• Explore various items and information from the trip, possibly manipulating data and materials in a final project or discussion. • Prepare a statistical analysis of the causes of homelessness, with predictions about the future of homelessness in the United States. • Compare and contrast homelessness in the United States with homelessness in other countries.
Visual/ Spatial	• View images, especially those created by the homeless. • Create a piece of art (drawing, painting, sculpture) depicting the plight of the homeless. • Create a map that illustrates concentrations of homeless people in the United States.
Bodily/ Kinesthetic	• Reenact scenes involving the life of a homeless person. • Plan a food and blanket drive in your school, then distribute to the homeless in your city. • Explore the effects of homelessness on the human body.
Musical/ Rhythmic	• Study and learn songs about improving life in America (such as those by Bob Dylan or Tracy Chapman), including examples by contemporary songwriters. • Write songs about the plight of the homeless. • Explore the role of music in a homeless person's life. • Interview a street musician.
Interpersonal	• Work as a group within the unit. • Brainstorm solutions to homelessness in small groups and create a plan of action for your class based on these solutions. • Divide into groups that each research a different aspect of homelessness (such as health care, education, causes, and so forth), then present information to the class.
Intrapersonal	• Make individual choices during personal exploration time on the virtual field trip. • Write an essay about what it would be like to be homeless. • Write a story about what the world would be like if everyone had a home (including the conditions necessary for this to be possible).
Naturalist	• Make a timeline concerning social justice and social action in America, starting at the beginning of the 20th century. • Explore the relationship of homeless people to the physical environment (such as why many choose to stay in or near cities; how they deal with climate; and so forth). • Explore the relationships between homeless people and their companion animals.

Appendix

In This Chapter

- A Quick Introduction to the Internet (p. 122)
- The Multiple Intelligences: An Overview (p. 128)
- Blank Template for Creating Your Own Field Trips (p. 129)

Appendix

This appendix contains the following supplemental material:

- a brief introduction to the Internet, for those unfamiliar with this technology
- an overview of the multiple intelligences, which play a large role in all of the field trips
- a blank template you can reproduce and use to create your own field trips

A Quick Introduction to the Internet

The following section is for those who have limited experience using the Internet, or for those who are rather uncomfortable at the prospect of having to use this technology. The purpose is to introduce the various terminologies and a basic understanding of how the technology operates.

One of the greatest hindrances to incorporating the Internet into the classroom is teacher *cyberphobia*—fear of things online (Mandel 1999). Cyberphobia is a real phenomenon. It causes teachers who are experienced and proficient in all other aspects of their teaching to avoid every use of technological resources because of their basic discomfort, which stems from a lack of experience. I have witnessed many an Internet-connected classroom PC being used for nothing more than games or for a school-designated reading- or math-assessment program, simply because the teacher was cyberphobic. The fact is, teachers generally will not use what they do not understand, or what they feel uncomfortable using. Nor will they force themselves to get over this discomfort unless they see the personal benefit of the innovation.

There are two basic ways you can rid yourself of cyberphobia:

- Actively see the value of integrating the Internet into the curricula as a means to both enrich the students' learning experience and ultimately make your professional life easier.
- Experience how easy it is to navigate the Internet.

The fact is that it is easier to navigate the Internet than to operate a VCR. In addition, once you learn a few easy Internet tools, you will be able to locate educational websites within minutes (see chapter 3).

To help you become comfortable with the Internet, this section introduces the basic terminology of the Internet and how the Internet functions. For a more detailed discussion, see *Social Studies in the Cyberage: Applications with Cooperative Learning* (Mandel 1999).

Servers

The most basic part of the Internet is the server, also known as an *Internet Service Provider,* or *ISP* for short. The server is the mechanism that connects you to the Internet. The easiest way to understand how the Internet works is to think of it as being similar to your phone system. The server would be synonymous with your local phone company, the organization that provides you with your basic phone service. You sign up once, and you never have to think of it again, unless you decide to change your basic service.

The same situation occurs with your server. The server is the company that provides you with your basic Internet services. Servers come in a number of forms. Some are large national companies such as AOL, Earthlink, or a phone company–based service. Others are small private companies that serve only local customers. Still others are educational services, often operated by school systems, that offer their services to teachers for free. If your school is hooked up to the Internet, you probably don't have a choice of servers. However, you should become familiar with the various types of servers if you wish to set up the Internet in your own home. Knowing the relative features of each type of server will also help you to evaluate student and community Internet access if you choose to use outside resources for all or part of the field trip. Although all types of servers connect you to the Internet, there are some major differences among them (see Pros and Cons of Internet Service Providers on following page).

Browsers

Browsers are the software that allows your computer to operate on the Internet. The server connects you online; the browser allows you to work. The two major types of browser software are Netscape and Microsoft Internet Explorer. Both of these programs are virtually the same, with only minor stylistic variations. In addition, both Netscape and Internet Explorer are free to all educators.

The browser is similar to your long distance phone service. Once you set up your service, you never have to worry about it again, unless you change your long distance carrier. For example, every time you dial a "1" on your phone, you are connected to your long distance carrier. Every time you connect to the Internet, you connect through your browser.

Pros and Cons of Internet Service Providers

Service Providers	Positive Aspects	Negative Aspects
Large National Companies	• Services provided by large companies are easy to use, especially for first-time users.	• You can access the Internet only through their systems, which slows down your access time considerably. This is especially true when you have to wait for all of their advertisements to download before you can proceed to online material (unless you're lucky enough to have a DSL, cable modem, or other fast connection). • Tech support is often impersonal.
Small Private Companies	• Small companies may struggle to keep their equipment up to date for their customers. • They generally have easy, quick Internet connections without advertisements. • Tech support is more personalized and easy to use.	• They may charge a couple dollars more than other services. However, beware of the companies that charge a "special" low yearly fee—you may never hear from them again, especially if you need tech support.
Educational Entities	• Educational entities often supply their services free (or at a greatly reduced cost) for educators.	• The fact that they are operated by non-profit entities makes upgrade of equipment problematic, thereby causing delays for teachers during peak evening hours. • They usually offer tech support only during school hours—when you are working.

Plug-ins

As technology improves exponentially, especially online technology, those who design computer systems and software are faced with a serious dilemma: design new updated systems and software every couple of months or somehow discover a way to easily upgrade current systems and software to take advantage of online technological breakthroughs. The result: *plug-ins*.

Plug-ins are basically extensions to your current software that enable your Internet browser (such as Netscape or Internet Explorer) to take advantage of new technological innovations. For example, new software is developed every month for improving online audio and video files, but the browsers are not set up to handle these new programs. Therefore, plug-ins are developed to integrate with your current browser, allowing you to use the new technology (such as online audio and video software) on a particular website without having to purchase new software.

How do you know when you need a plug-in? How do you acquire and install plug-ins? In most cases, the site tells you. For example, if you go to a site that requires a plug-in in order to use or view a particular file, you will often get a message of this sort:

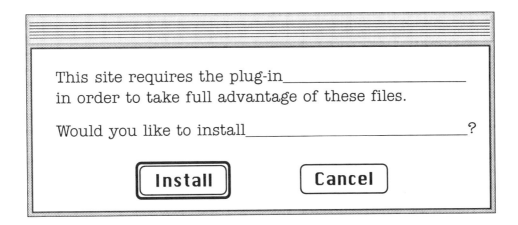

All you have to do is select the "install" button to install the plug-in in your system. In some cases, you will need to download the plug-in before installing it, but the site where you find the plug-in will usually walk you through any additional steps. Plug-in installation is extremely user-friendly.

As you prepare a virtual field trip, you should investigate whether plug-ins are required on any steps of the trip. If plug-ins are necessary on a particular site, you need to determine the following:

- Do the student computers already have the plug-ins installed?
- Is the plug-in material necessary for the virtual field trip?

The second question is very important. Often a plug-in simply enables you to see or hear an extraneous video or recording—features that may not be critical to the website. You need to assess the importance of the material versus the extra time and effort of installing the plug-in on all student computers.

URLs and Addresses

URLs (short for *Uniform Resource Locators*) and addresses are synonymous terms. They are the "phone numbers" of the Internet. These are the locators for all websites. Similar to a phone number, these letters and numbers have to be exactly correct for a connection to occur.

URLs are a remnant of the archaic UNIX system on which the Internet was originally based, hence the long, cumbersome string of letters, numbers, and symbols. However, once you familiarize yourself with the various parts of the address, URLs are quite easy to use and understand. Following is an example of a URL from a fictional educational site:

http://www.socialstudiesstuff.edu/~civilwar

This URL is actually composed of five separate and distinct parts, each of which has a specific meaning and importance:

http://   www   socialstudiesstuff   .edu   /~civilwar

http://

This part of the URL is used less and less in advertisements and in the general publicity about Internet sites. In fact, with most browsers, you don't have to include it to connect to the site you wish to use. The website listings in this book do not include this part of the address.

www.

This part of the URL is also gradually dropping from usage. These letters stand for *World Wide Web*. Whereas only a few years ago, many different types of Internet sources were available (the World Wide Web being but one of them), nowadays virtually every site you go to will be a World Wide Web site, thereby making the "www." superfluous. Be aware that many sites are dropping the "www" from their URLs. Do not assume that every Internet address automatically includes it.

socialstudiesstuff

This section of the URL is the most important section because it contains the primary information of the site. In the URLs of large well-known sites, or of commercial entities, this section usually consists of the name of the company or subject matter. As a result, you can often guess the URL based on the name of a site (see example on page 127).

.edu

This part of the URL tells you the type of site. There are only a handful of these suffixes, although more are being approved at this time (mostly in the online auction, media, and commercial areas). The basic sites that you will discover in your Internet use will be of the following types:

URL Type of Site Designation

.com or .cc	commercial sites
.edu	educational sites
.org	nonprofit organization sites
.gov	official government sites
.net	small private servers, usually personal sites
.uk, .il, and so forth	sites originating in a foreign country—each country outside the United States has its own code: for example ".uk" is United Kingdom; ".il" is Israel

/~civilwar

This part of the URL is not always present. This section refers to a particular file in the overall website. In our example, it would lead to the "Civil War" page of the Social Studies Stuff site. Think of this part of the URL as being similar to a phone extension. If you have someone's extension number, you can reach that particular office more quickly. If you do not have the extension, you can still reach the office you want by going through a receptionist. The website works in a similar fashion. By using "/~civilwar" you can reach that information immediately. If you do not have it, you can still access the same page by going through a link on the opening page (home page) of the Internet site.

You can use this information about the various sections of URLs to locate sites when you may not know the address offhand. For example, if you want to locate the official NASA website, you could guess at the URL, using the acronym for NASA and the knowledge that it is a government agency:

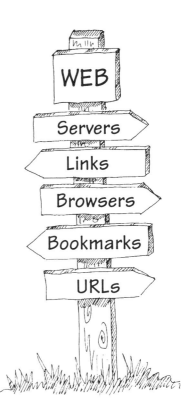

http://www.nasa.gov

This system does not work in all instances, but it does in many, especially when you want to locate large corporations, educational organizations, or government sources.

Links and Bookmarks

Links and bookmarks (also called *favorites*) act like the speed dial buttons on your phone. Instead of having to type a long URL every time you want an online site, you simply point and click on a link or bookmark and go directly to the location.

There are two ways to recognize a link:

- The words of the link are a different color from the text (usually blue) and underlined. After you have clicked on that link at least once, the color changes, usually to purple.

- In most systems and software, when you touch a link, the arrow cursor turns into a hand with a finger pointed. This is especially helpful when you come across a graphic that has been set up as a link. (You click on the image just as you would click on a text link.)

Bookmarks (or favorites) operate in a similar fashion and are extremely important for the classroom teacher. As with links, bookmarks also act like speed dial buttons on your phone. By following links throughout the Internet, you will often discover websites that you would like to use again. Unfortunately, after going from link to link, you may not remember how you originally discovered the site, thereby making its future use virtually impossible without writing down the URL, a tedious process with a large probability of error. Bookmarks allow you to create a permanent link to that site on your personal computer.

Creating bookmarks is simple. When you find an Internet site that you want to save, go up to the bookmarks (or favorites) menu, select "Add Bookmark," and release. The next time you open that menu, the site you saved will be listed in that location. Now when you want to use that site, all you have to do is open the bookmarks menu, scroll to the name of that site, and you will be immediately connected to that Internet location. No typing in the URL; no worrying about where you originally discovered the site.

The Multiple Intelligences: An Overview

Following is a brief description of the eight current multiple intelligences. For a full description of each of the intelligences, including detailed explanations of how teachers can apply multiple-intelligence theory to their curricula, please see Thomas Armstrong's *Multiple Intelligences in the Classroom* (2000).

Verbal/Linguistic
Core components: sensitivity to the sounds, structure, meanings, and functions of words and language

Logical/Mathematical
Core components: sensitivity to, and capacity to discern, logical or numerical patterns; ability to handle long chains of reasoning

Visual/Spatial
Core components: capacity to perceive accurately the visual-spatial world and to perform transformations of one's initial perceptions

Bodily/Kinesthetic
Core components: ability to control one's body movements and to handle objects skillfully

Musical/Rhythmic
Core components: ability to produce and appreciate rhythm, pitch, and timbre; ability to distinguish and appreciate different forms of musical expression

Interpersonal
Core components: capacity to discern and respond appropriately to the moods, temperaments, motivations, and desires of other people

Intrapersonal
Core components: access to one's own emotional life and the ability to discriminate among one's emotions; knowledge of personal strengths and weaknesses

Naturalist
Core components: sensitivity to the natural world and ability to classify and see connections and patterns within the plant and animal kingdoms by distinguishing among members of a species; recognizing the existence of neighboring species; and charting out the relationships among several species

Blank Template for Creating Your Own Field Trips

You may reproduce the forms on the following pages if you wish to create your own virtual field trips. Simply follow the examples throughout part 2 of this book. Reproduce enough copies of the Internet Sites chart (page 131) to cover the number of websites you locate.

Virtual Field Trip _____

 As a result of this virtual field trip, the students will

Subtopics
-
-
-
-

Integration into the Unit

- Focus of learning activities before the trip:

- Focus of learning activities after the trip:

Internet Sites (Sorted by Subtopic)

Subtopic	Title of Site and URL	Notes about Site

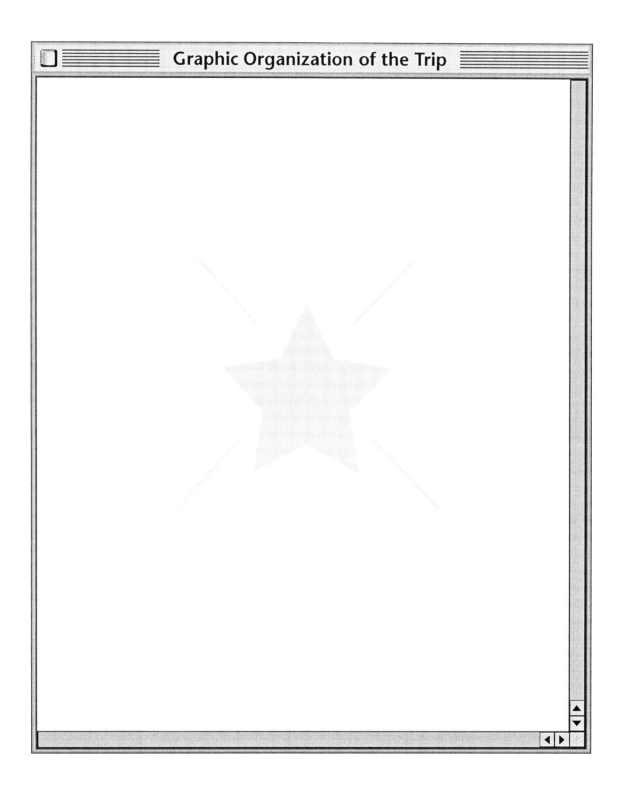

Using the Multiple Intelligences

Intelligence	Activities
Verbal/ Linguistic	
Logical/ Mathematical	
Visual/ Spatial	
Bodily/ Kinesthetic	
Musical/ Rhythmic	
Interpersonal	
Intrapersonal	
Naturalist	

Final Projects

-
-
-
-

Bibliography

Armstrong, T. 2000. *Multiple Intelligences in the Classroom.* 2nd Edition. Alexandria, Va.: Association for Supervision and Curriculum Development.

Dede, C. 1997. "Rethinking How to Invest in Technology." *Educational Leadership,* 55(3), 12–16.

Dewey, J. 1959. "The Child and the Curriculum." In M. Dworkin (Ed.). *Dewey on Education.* New York: Bureau of Publications, Teachers College, Columbia University.

Eisner, E. 1979. *The Educational Imagination.* New York: Macmillan Publishing.

Gilster, P. 1997. "A New Digital Literacy: A Conversation with Paul Gilster." *Educational Leadership,* 55(3), 6–11.

Krepel, W. J., and C. R. Duvall. 1981. *Field Trips: A Guide for Planning and Conducting Educational Experiences.* Washington, D.C.: National Education Association.

Mandel, S. 1999. *Social Studies in the Cyberage: Applications with Cooperative Learning.* Arlington Heights, Ill.: Skylight Training and Publishing, Inc.

———. 2000. *Virtual Field Trips in the Cyberage: A Content Mapping Approach.* Arlington Heights, Ill.: Skylight Training and Publishing, Inc.

Rudman, C. L. 1994. "A Review of the Use and Implementation of Science Field Trips." *School Science and Mathematics,* 94(3), 138–41.

Index

communities, field trips
    adapting (to age levels), 50
    careers, 57–61
    families and culture, 52–6
    integration (into classroom), 52, 57, 62
    multiple intelligences, using, 56, 61, 66
    organization, graphical, 54, 59, 64
    origins, 62–6
    projects, final, 55, 60, 65
    websites, 51, 53, 58, 63
Cybertrips in Social Studies, organization of, 8–9

evaluation
    definition of, 31
    goals, matching to the, 32–4, 35 (chart)
    what is, 30–1
experiential education, importance of, 5–6

field trips. *See also* virtual field trips
    definition of, 5
    Internet, limited or no access to, 14–5, 17–8
    scheduling, 13–4
    troubleshooting, 16 (chart)

history, field trips
    adapting (to age levels), 68
    ancient Greece, 91–5
    Civil War, 80–5
    Crusades, 96–100
    Declaration of Independence, 75–9
    French Revolution, 101–6
    Great Depression, 86–90
    integration (into classroom), 71, 75, 80, 86, 91, 96, 101
    multiple intelligences, using, 74, 79, 85, 90, 95, 100, 106
    organization, graphical of, 73, 77, 83, 88, 93, 98, 104
    projects, final, 74, 78, 84, 89, 94, 99, 105
    states (individual), 70–4
    websites, 69, 72, 76, 81–2
humanities, field trips
    adapting (to age levels), 108
    democracy (concept course), 110–4
    homeless (social action), 115–9
    integration (into classroom), 110, 115
    multiple intelligences, using, 114, 119
    organization, graphical, 112, 117
    projects, final, 113, 118
    websites, 109, 111, 116

Internet. *See also* websites
    browsers, 123–4
    integrating (into classroom), 12–8
    introduction to, 122–8
    links and bookmarks, 128
    locating material, 21–7
    servers, 123
    URLs and addresses, 125–7

multiple intelligences, overview of, 128–9

search engines and directories, 22–3

URLs (uniform resource locators), providing for students, 42

virtual field trip. *See also* websites
    adapting (ways to), 50, 68, 108
    Ancient Greece, 91–5
    careers, 57–61
    Civil War, 80–5
    Crusades, 96–100
    Declaration of Independence, 75–9
    democracy (concept course), 110–4
    evaluation of, 33–4, 35 (chart)
    example of, 40–1
    families and culture, 52–6
    French Revolution, 101–6
    Great Depression, 86–90
    homeless (social action), 115–9
    how to use, 12–3
    origins, 62–6
    overview, 39, 40–1(chart)
    setting up a, 38–9
    states (individual), 70–4, 75
    template for creating, 129–134
    websites, 7
    what is, 6–7

web pages,
    creating an original, 43–4
    sample of, 44, 45 (chart)
websites
    ancient Greece, 92
    bookmarking, 43
    careers, 58
    comprehensive subject matter, 25–6
    Civil War, 81–2
    Crusades, 97
    Declaration of Independence, 76
    democracy, 111
    education (general), 24–5
    families and culture, 53
    French Revolution, 102–3
    Great Depression, 87
    guestbooks, 26–7
    history, 42, 51, 69
    homeless, 116
    humanities, 109
    origins, 63
    sites, no longer available, 21–2
    states (individual), 72
    virtual field trip, 7
    World War II, 4–5